ETHNIC CHRONOLOGY SERIES
NUMBER 30

The Greeks in America

1528-1977

A Chronology & Fact Book

Compiled and edited by

Melvin Hecker & Heike Fenton

1978
OCEANA PUBLICATIONS, INC.
DOBBS FERRY, NEW YORK

Library of Congress Cataloging in Publication Data
Main entry under title:

The Greeks in America, 1528-1977.

    (Ethnic chronology series)
    Bibliography: p.
    Includes index.
    SUMMARY: A chronology of the Greeks in America
accompanied by pertinent documents.
    1. Greek Americans — History — Chronology. 2. Greek
Americans — History — Sources. [1. Greek Americans —
History] I. Hecker, Melvin, 1946-　II. Fenton, Heike.
III. Series.
E184.G7G73　　　973'.04'893　　　77-93976
ISBN 0-379-00531-X

Manufactured in the United States of America

To

Robert A. Fenton
H.F.

and

Monica G-S Hecker
M.H.

Seek not, my soul, the life of the immortals; but enjoy to
the full the resources that are within they reach.

Pindar 518-438 BC
Pythian Odes III

TABLE OF CONTENTS

INTRODUCTION

The United States of America has developed into the world power that it is today because of the diversified background of its people. The various nationality groups with their different religions and traditions blended into a creative force that has spurred America's continued progress and prosperity. The Greek influence in the United States is unique and, however slight at first, has been formative throughtout most of the country's growth. In this volume we identify five periods which encompass the historical development of the Greek population in America. The first period covers the years 1528 to 1821, a time when Greece was under the domination of the Ottoman rulers. It was a period of little movement and of few records which could provide information on those who left their homeland in search of adventure in the New World.

After the Greek War of Independence from Turkey had been fought and won, more Greeks began disembarking in the United States. This marks the beginning of the second period that extends from 1821 to 1890. But, it was not until the early 1890s that the Greeks truly began to arrive in significant numbers. Once their exodus had started, it grew rapidly. The increase in tempo delineates the beginning of the third period which lasted until 1921.

Up to this point, the vast majority of Greek immigrants were men who had left their families in Greece to come to the United States seeking their fortune. They settled chiefly in major cities, industrial centers, and mill towns where they formed their own temporary communities. These immigrants did not expect to stay in America; they came to earn a bit of money and return home. The early Greek arrivals were a hard-working group who often lived in crowded tenements, but who always strove to improve their lot, and sent most of their hard-earned wages to their families back home.

This period of ultranationalism began yielding to the pressures of Americanization at the beginning of the 1920s. As the Greeks adjusted to life in the United States and the economic situation in Greece deteriorated, the Greek immigrant realized that repatriation was a dream and that making a home for his family in the United States was more to his advantage. The change in attitude was slow, and was accompanied by open conflict in the Greek communities over the question of Americanization. AHEPA and GAPA represented the major rival factions during a very divisive period. Topographically, Greece is a variable country, and throughout her long history, her people have lived in fractious rivalry, divided according to their regions or islands, and subdivided by their political convictions. The Greek feuds did not end when they came to America, they were taken up in their newly formed communities.

The drive toward Americanization resulted in a great number of Greek aliens applying for United States citizenship. Naturalization reached its peak in the late 1920s, tapered off somewhat through the 1930s, then regained momentum again in the early 1940s. The Greek immigrant was being transformed into an American of Hellenic descent.

The final period, extending from the 1940s to the present, is defined by the term Philhellenism. Having worked hard to achieve a place in the United States, the American Greek felt an awakening need to express himself in new ways, and to press closer to his mother country. Both of these trends, on which the Second World War undoubtedly had its effects, have persisted and evolved. The American Greek is branching out and exhibiting talent in many fields, including the arts and sciences. The resurgence of the Greek-American's concern for the mother country is reflected in a new political awareness and his involvement with lobbying Congress on behalf of his special interests.

In the pages that follow we have presented information which we believe will give the reader an objective picture of the Hellenic presence in the United States. In Part I, the Chronology, we have selected key dates and events to indicate the progress that the Greeks have made in this country. The Documents section, Part II of this volume, provides the reader with a more in-depth look at a selection of the significant events referred to in the Chronology. For those researchers interested in exploring the subject matter further, the annotated bibliography at the end of the book should prove to be a most useful guide.

Our appreciation is extended to George Hatziaounoui of the Greek Information Service in New York for providing us with some initial leads, and to the staff of the Public Affairs Department of the Greek Archdiocese of North and South America both for their interest in this book and for supplying its editors with important reference materials. We should also like to thank Mrs. Marieta Toby of Mercy College Library for her patient assistance in this research effort.

The Editors

EARLY IMMIGRATION
1528 - 1821

With the exception of the accounts of the New Smyrna Colony, there are few records to be found about Greek immigrants to America during the early years of colonization. We may be certain, however, that individual Greeks who are not mentioned here, following a true spirit of adventurism, in the service of Spain or on merchant ships, found their way to the New World.

1528 A Greek by the name of Theodoros arrived with the Spaniards at Tarpon Springs, Florida. He was the first Greek to land in America. Alvar Nunez de Cabeza mentioned him on several occasions in his account of the expedition. Theodoros had gone inland with some seemingly friendly Indians to get water, and when he did not return, the stranded Spaniards were despondent over the loss.

1592 Apostolos Valerianos, called Juan de Fuca by the Spaniards, discovered the Strait of Juan de Fuca while in the service of Spain. The Fuca Strait is located between Washington State and Vancouver.

1652 Konopios, who had come from Crete, established the first Greek coffee house in New England.

Dr. John Turnbull set off with more than 1400 immigrants, mostly Minorcans, Italians, and some 500 Greeks, to America to settle on his extensive land-holdings in the wilderness of Florida. At this time, Florida was under British rule. Turnbull had received generous help from his king and government with his colonization scheme.

The new settlement, located on the Mosquitoes inlet, was named New Smyrna after the birthplace of Dr. Turnbull's Greek wife, Gracia Dura Bin.

Turnbull's original plan was to bring five hundred Greeks to New Smyrna. But, by the time he left the Mediterranean, he was transporting more than 1400 people. During the rough sea voyage over three hundred of the emigrants died, and when the settlers finally arrived at their destination, they found only a wilderness and insufficient provisions for their large number.

Because of the extreme hardships, excessive labor, short supplies of food, malaria, and maltreatment by their overseers that rapidly decreased their numbers, the settlers rebelled under the leadership of the Italian Carlo Forni. About three hundred of them captured a ship that had arrived from St. Augustine and tried to escape. The boat was spotted a few days later, and they abandoned their plan. Thirty-five of these desperate people still tried to get away in a small boat, but they were caught later.

Turnbull had asked for military assistance in order to subdue the rebels. Even after the revolt had been put down, a small garrison was stationed at New Smyrna. Smyrna.

Governor James Grant, who was a sympathetic supporter of the new settlement, wrote to England at the end of the year that the New Smyrna Colony had lost about three hundred old people and children to sickness.

1769   January. The trial of the rebels took place in St. Augustine. Three of them were sentenced to death, among them Elia Medici, a Greek from Corsica who had killed a cow. His death sentence, however, was not carried out. In accordance with British law at that time, he was freed after he had executed the other two rebels.

Turnbull had made contracts with all his settlers, according to which they could not separate from his service for six to ten years. At the end of the specified period, each settler was to receive one hundred acres for himself and fifty acres for each member of his family. Consequently, even those who would have dared to leave did not want to lose what they had struggled for so desperately. Only the most hopeless ones and those who were strong enough left and went to St. Augustine at this time.

Twice during the year of 1769 Governor Grant sent food and supplies to New Smyrna to help the starving colony.

1770   Two years after the arrival of the colonists, only 628 were left.

1771   After Governor Grant resigned, the British home office decided not to support New Smyrna any longer.

1777   A small village had been established by this time at New Smyrna. There were stores, a windmill, 145 houses, indigo works, large wharfs, canals, and boats.

A deep animosity existed between Governor Patrick Tonyn, who had succeeded Grant, and Turnbull. The two men had begun to quarrel almost as soon as Tonyn had arrived. Governor Tonyn employed ruthless tactics against Turnbull, and after having discredited him, claimed that Turnbull had never intended to give the colonists the land he had promised them because the original land grants stipulated the settlers had to be Protestants. Encouraged by the governor's disregard of the courts and Turnbull's neglect of New Smyrna, because he was too involved fighting Tonyn, the whole settlement moved to St. Augustine despite the protests of Turnbull's attorneys.

July. The courts ordered Dr. Turnbull to set all of his settlers free. By November all of them had left for St. Augustine.

Over one hundred women and children were begging around the governor's house in St. Augustine. About ten deaths a week occured among these settlers. Men, who were still healthy, were taken into the Rangers, and the others were left to build hovels for themselves on small lots assigned to them north of St. Augustine. They had no money to buy supplies for farming, and most of them existed as fishermen along the shore.

The failure of the New Smyrna Colony can be blamed largely on the fight between Turnbull and Tonyn, the disregard of human consideration for the unfortunate settlers, and perhaps just as importantly, on the wilderness that surrounded them.

1778   By the end of January, 419 of the settlers from New Smyrna were still alive in St. Augustine; about 128 of these were children born in New Smyrna.

John Geannopoulos taught school in St. Augustine.
His house, the oldest school house in America, has
been restored and still stands.

June. D. Ypsilantis led Greek volunteers in the Battle
of Monmouth, New Jersey, during the American Revolution. There is no record of their origin, but perhaps
some of them had come from New Smyrna and St.
Augustine.

1783 When Florida was returned to the Spaniards, according
to the Treaty of Paris, 460 survivors from New Smyrna,
including those born in Florida, who were still strug-
gling in St. Augustine, signed a memorandum stating
that they would gladly remain under Spanish rule.

Russian and Greek missionaries founded the Greek
Orthodox Mission in Alaska.

1784 The Greek Russian Eustotius Juanobitos Delaref, who
had settled in Alaska, became governor of Kontiac
Island.

1805 Alexander Dimitry was born in New Orleans. His
grandmother had emigrated from Greece and arrived
in New Orleans in 1760. He became the first English
editor of the New Orleans Bee, published in French.
He was a well-known teacher, editor, and diplomat,
and was the first state superintendant of education.
President James Buchanan appointed him minister to
Costa Rica in 1859. Under Jefferson Davis, president of the Confederate States, he was chief of the
post office department. He died in 1883.

1821 When Florida was traded for Cuba by an arrangement
made between the United States and Spain, landhold-
ings of the former New Smyrna settlers and their descendants amounted to 48,956 acres.

SCATTERED IMMIGRATION AFTER THE
WAR OF INDEPENDENCE
1821 - 1890

On March 25, 1821, Archbishop Germanos raised the
Cross for Freedom to begin Greece's rebellion against
Turkish rule. Greece had been conquered by Turkey
during the fifteenth century and had since been part
of the Ottoman Empire. For almost four centuries
Greeks had accepted their fate, but at the outbreak
of the nineteenth century Greek nationalism was revived. In 1821 her people rebelled, and the War of
Independence began.

The bloody and often hopeless war against Turkey received much attention in the New World, especially
after the massacre of Chios, where Turks murdered
30,000 of the inhabitants. Americans took up the
cause of Greece, and many joined her forces, either
fighting for her or helping those that were left homeless or without families. One of the most prominent
American fighters for Greece was Dr. Samuel Gridley Howe, who brought many Greek orphans to
America.

1822   During the Greek War of Independence, President
        James Monroe was one of the first to address Congress
        on behalf of the Greeks and to ask for support in her
        fight. All over the United States relief funds were
        organized to help Greece.

1828   Evangelides Apostolides Sophocles arrived in Boston
        at the age of twenty-four.

1832   George Musalas Colvokoressis became midshipman
        in the United States Navy after graduating from the
        Military Academy of Norwich, Connecticut. He had
        been brought to America in 1822 after the massacre
        of Chios.

1833   The United States recognized the sovereignty of the
        Kingdom of Greece.

1836   A treaty establishing diplomatic relations between
        Greece and America was signed.

1841   President John Tyler appointed Photius Kavasales
                (Fisk) a chaplain in the United States Navy. After
                his confirmation by the Senate, he served on the
                USS Columbia and the USS Raritan.

1842   Evangelides Apostolides Sophocles became professor
                of Ancient, Byzantine, and Modern Greek at Harvard
                University in Cambridge, Massachusetts. Among his
                numerous writings, he is particularly acclaimed for
                the Greek Lexicon of the Roman and Byzantine Periods
                from B.C. 146 to A.D. 1100.

1845   Gregorios Perdikaris, who was orphaned during the
                Greek War of Independence and had been brought to
                America by missionaries, was appointed United
                States consul in Athens, Greece.

                The Annual Report of the Commissioner General of
                Immigration stated that only one Greek had arrived
                in New York that year.

1850   John M. Rodonaki came to America. He was Greek
                consul in Boston for twenty-two years. When he
                died, he left the largest part of his estate to the
                Boston Art Museum.

1857   Spyros Bazanos opened the Peleponnesus, the first
                Greek restaurant in New York City.

                Nicholas Peppas was the first Greek to settle in
                Chicago.

1858   Two Greeks arrived in the United States according
                to immigration statistics.

1859   Consul General Demetrios Botassi came to New
                York.

1860   During the Civil War George Musalas Colvokoressis
                took command of the USS Supply and captured the
                blockade runner Stephen Hart, which was carrying
                ammunition for the Confederacy.

1863   Commander Colvokoressis took charge of the USS
                Saratoga. He was awarded two citations and a
                commendation by Secretary of the Navy Gideon Wells

for his outstanding achievements during the Civil
War.

1864   A Greek Orthodox congregation was formed in New
Orleans, Louisiana, by Greek cotton merchants.

Joannes Jelivergos Zachos's Phonic Primer and Reader
for adults was published. Zachos had been brought
to America as a ten-year old by Dr. Samuel Gridley
Howe and served as assistant surgeon in the Union
Army during the Civil War.

1865   The Reverend Agapius Honcurenko arrived from Greece
to take charge of the first Greek Orthodox congregation in New Orleans.

Captain John Colvokoressis retired from the United
States Navy.

1866   Construction of Holy Trinity, the first Greek Orthodox church in the United States, was begun. It was
located at 1222 Dorgenois Street in New Orleans, Louisiana. Inaugural services were held in July 1877.

1868   Michael Anagnos, who was born in Epiros in 1837,
came to Boston, Massachusetts, with Dr. Samuel
Gridley Howe. Anagnos began teaching Latin and Greek
at the Perkins Institution for the Blind, founded by
Dr. Howe.

1870   After marrying Dr. Howe's daughter, Julia Romana, Anagnos gradually took over the direction of the Perkins
Institution.

Greek sailors settled in Seattle, Washington.

The Greek foreign minister, A. Romanos, wrote to the
American minister in Athens, A.S. Hardy, that "American citizenship of Greek immigrants cannot be recognized in Greece unless they have requested and ob-
tained the prescribed permission of the Government
and discharged their military obligations to the country
of their origin." This attitude by the Greek government did not change for many years to come.

1871   Joannes Zelivergos Zachos became curator of Cooper

Union in New York City.

1872   George Musalas Colvokoressis was shot by thieves
        in Bridgeport, Connecticut, while on a business trip.

        At the time of Dr. Howe's death, Anagnos became
        director of the Perkins Institution. His work and ded-
        ication made him one of the most beloved and most
        outstanding men of his time.

1877   The first Greek newspaper to comment on Greek emi-
        gration was Sphaira (The Globe) of Piraeus. It mention-
        ed that Greek immigration to the United States began
        when about fourteen men from Tsintsinon sailed for
        America. Obviously, the journalist was not familiar
        with earlier emigration.

1880   Greek immigration to the United States increased
        significantly.

1881   The Greco-Slavic Brotherhood, a religious organization,
        was founded in Chicago, Illinois.

        During the 1880s Turkey passed a law making mili-
        tary service compulsory for all Christian minorities,
        thus causing substantial emigration of Greek Ortho-
        dox residents in Asia Minor.

1882   The federal government of the United States assumed
        control of immigration. The period following this change
        was called the "Era of New Immigration." This date
        also coincides with the arrival of large numbers of
        Greeks in America. By the 1890s it had reached size-
        able proportions. This exodus can be blamed largely
        on the precarious economic conditions prevailing in
        Greece during these years. The new arrivals were al-
        most exclusively men seeking employment in the "land
        of opportunity." Few of them planned to stay perman-
        ently, as most of them were simply looking for a
        temporary solution to supporting their families who
        had stayed behind in Greece.

        Although some of these immigrants would eventually
        return to their homeland, the majority of them stayed.
        Thus, a new phenomenon on the American immigration
        scene was created, namely communities that were

predominantly male. During the first twenty to thirty years of Greek mass immigration, this ethnic group had the highest percentage of unmarried men.

1882   Immigration reports showed that 125 Greek men and one Greek woman arrived in America this year.

1885   A. Evangelides, editor of Eagle and Citizen, was e-lected Democratic representative of Brooklyn, New York.

According to United States Immigration Reports, 172 Greeks arrived in the United States.

The first store owned by a Greek, a florist, opened in New York City.

1886   When asked to report about Greek immigration to the United States, the American consul in Athens, William H. Moffett, wrote that there was "None." Evidently, he was unaware of the facts.

1887   The commissioner general of immigration in his "Annual Reports" listed 313 new Greek arrivals.

Consul Moffett, aware of the mounting numbers of Greeks seeking to emigrate to the United States, wrote an anxious note to the State Department.

The number of Greeks arriving in America had in-creased to 782.

The Greek press began to publish letters by Greek immigrants in the United States describing the hard-ships the Greek immigrants faced in the new land. Since generally letters from immigrants glorified their achievements rather than referred to their failures, it is conceivable that this was an attempt to stem emigration from Greece.

One-hundred and fifty Greeks, who had just landed in New York, were engaged for railroad construction work in Quebec, Canada. A week later the company failed, and these men were stranded. Enduring much hardship in a strange and wild land, they made their way to a village in Maine. The people of the village

helped them to get to Boston. The incident is remarkable only in so far as it refers to a large group
of immigrants. Newly arrived Greeks were often ex-
ploited, especially because of language difficulties,
and most often by Greeks who were already established in the United States.

Consul Moffett, now familiar with the facts, was a-
larmed by the increase in emigration. He requested
the State Department to place restrictions on the
issuance of visas in order to reduce the number of
emigrating Greeks.

1889

The number of Greek immigrants arriving in America
this year was 158.

Jane Adams founded Hull House in Chicago, Illinois.
Located in the center of Greek town, it was well
known for its charitable, cultural, and social works
and facilities. It was especially important to the
Greek immigrants in the area who depended on Hull
House to orient themselves in their new community.

Grace Abbott founded and became director of the
League for the Protection of Immigrants in Chicago,
an organization that did much to assist immigrants.

PERIOD OF SYSTEMATIC IMMIGRATION
1891 - 1921

The failure of the Greek currency in addition to the
already precarious economic conditions prevailing in
Greece, led to the mass exodus of Greeks seeking
their fortune in the United States.

At the end of the Balkan Wars, 1912, Greece became
swelled with refugees which her already overburdened
economy could not sustain. Once again the numbers of
Greeks emigrating reached large proportions. Almost
a half million Greeks came to America during this
period.

1891

For the first time Greek immigration to the United
States exceeded the one thousand people per annum
mark.

Prince George, oldest son of the Greek king, visited New York. He suggested to members of the Greek
community, numbering about five hundred at that
time, that they organize a Greek society.

The Hellenic Brotherhood of Athena, a Panhellenic
organization to promote the Greek Orthodox Church
in America and to preserve the Greek identity and
traditions, was founded in New York. Some years
later it sponsored the establishment of the first
Greek church in New York City and sent to Greece
for a priest.

Only a small number of Greeks had settled in Chicago, Illinois. By this date, there were only about
one hundred Greeks living in that city. Chicago,
however, was shortly to claim the largest Greek
settlement in the United States.

The Greeks in Chicago organized the Therapnean
Society, later called Lycurgos. Its purpose was to
establish a church and to arrange for a priest to come
from Greece to minister it.

The first Greek immigrants arrived in Lowell, Massachusetts, to work in the mills.

According to the "Annual Reports" of the Commissioner
General of Immigration, 1040 men and sixty-five
women emigrated from Greece to America this year.

Colonel Lucas M. Miller was nominated and elected
to the 52nd Congress of the United States, despite
the fact that he had neither wanted nor sought the
office. His speeches in Congress received considerable attention. Colonel Miller had been adopted and
brought to America as a boy by Colonel J. P. Miller,
who had served in the Greek army during the War of
Independence.

1892   Constantine Fasoularides published the first, though
short-lived, Greek newspaper of America in Boston,
Massachusetts. It was called Neos Kosmos (New
World.

Holy Trinity church of New York was founded. In 1896

it was chartered by a special act of the New York
legislature.

1893   Metropolitan Dionysios of Zakynthos was the first
Greek bishop to visit the United States. During his
stay he visited the older Greek communities.

The Greek flag was raised for the first time over
City Hall in New York to commemorate Greek Independence Day. About three hundred Greeks assembled
on Pearl Street to celebrate the event.

1894   About 125 Greeks were working in the mills in Lowell,
Massachusetts. The first coffee house, grocery
store, and bakery were established there. Several
years later, Lowell was to have one of the largest
and most active Greek communities in the United
States.

Solon J. Vlastos began publication of the newspaper
Atlantis in New York. It started as a four-page weekly, but by 1903 it had gained enough support to become a daily.

1895   After the Irish and French Canadians, the Greeks
were the third important group of immigrants to settle in Lowell, Mass. By now their colony numbered
about three hundred. They rented a hall to serve as
their church and hired a priest.

Likus & Drivas, the first Greek import company in
New York, was established.

1896   January. The New York Times reported that there
were over one thousand members in the different
Greek and Orthodox congregations in New York City.
The latest church to be established was the Syrian
branch on Washington Street, which had one hundred
communicants.

Over two thousand Greek immigrants arrived in
America during this year.

1897   When reports of war between Greece and Turkey
reached the Lowell community, they formed a volunteer company that went to Greece. Most of them re-

turned at the end of the short war. In many cases,
they brought back with them some of their friends and
relatives.

1898   The Therapnean Society (Lycurgos) in Chicago started
construction of the Holy Trinity church on Johnson
Street. It was the third Greek church in America and
the first church building owned by the society. Because of the intense factional strife in the church
community, which frequently resulted in much publi-
cized disputes and court battles, two more churches
were founded, dividing the Greek community in Chicago into three sections. The two churches built
later were St. Constantine on Michigan Avenue and
the Annunciation on La Salle Avenue.

1899   The Greek community in Boston, Massachusetts,
established a church.

1900   New developments led to a significant increase in the
flow of Greeks to the United States. These included
another drop in the Greek currency, crop failure, and
the arrival of political refugees from Turkey in an
influx that could not be supported by the weak Greek
economy. Almost four thousand Greeks arrived during
1900. At this time there were only eleven Greek
women for every one hundred Greek men in the United
States.

1901   The Greek community of Lowell, Mass., numbered
three thousand. It was located close to Market Street.
Most of these immigrants lived in overcrowded tenements, often nine or more in one room, maintaining
a co-operative housekeeping plan.

1902   April. The Athens correspondent of the London Times
reported that emigration, especially from Morea,
Peleponnesus, was increasing. During the last week
of March, six-hundred young men from Laconia and
Messenia left for New York. It was estimated that
since the beginning of the year about three thousand
had left. The cause of the exodus was believed to be
the poverty and political insecurity of the rural districts
owing to the exactions by outlaws and misgovernment
by local officials.

1902   The newspaper Hellas was published in New York
            City.

1903   The United States Legation in Athens informed the
            State Department that ". . . quite a large number of
            Greeks left Megara, Thebes, and Corinth for Boston,
            New York, St. Louis, and other American cities. Most
            of these immigrants were passed satisfactorily, but
            a number of them — notably those whose destination
            was St. Louis, were stopped and sent back..."

            The newspaper Greek Star was published in Chicago.

1904   In addition to the Greek churches in New York, Chi-
            cago, Boston, and New Orleans, there were now
            Greek churches planned in Lowell, Birmingham, San
            Francisco, Milwaukee, Newark, and Philadelphia.

            The first Greek church was built in Lowell at a cost
            of $80,000. The community leaders felt this excess-
            ive expenditure was justified as it would prevent the
            different factions from forming separate churches,
            and it would help to unite the community. The church
            was completed in 1908.

            Anagnos founded the National Union in Boston. He
            had plans to do the same in New York and Chicago,
            but they did not materialize.

            Socrates Xanthakys started publication of the Pan-
            Hellenic.

1905   April. The Greek community in Salt Lake City brought
            in the Reverend Archimandrite Parthenos Lymperopou-
            los who had been appointed by the Holy Synod of
            Greece. Shortly after his arrival, they began to build
            their church, the Holy Trinity.

            The Greek community in Atlanta, Georgia, bought a
            church.

            The number of Greek women immigrating to the United
            States increased. Greek girls, already betrothed to
            Greek men here, came with their families. The rise
            in Greek families also increased the need for the edu-
            cation of their children according to the old traditions.

Greek schools were established gradually in their communities.

A Greek community began to emerge in St. Louis, Missouri. By 1910 it had grown so much that it divided into two factions and had two separate churches. The city's Greek population was between five to six thousand at that time, and this number increased substantially during the winter months when Greek railroad workers came to the city.

John (Ionnes) M. Cocoris founded the sponge fishing industry in Tarpon Springs, Florida.

1906   Anagnos died while visiting Europe. His death was mourned by all Greeks and Americans who knew him.

Poraxenos began publication in New York and Athena in Chicago.

1906   There were about 100,000 Greeks in the United States. They belonged to various factions according to their native origin. The need to become coordinated under one major umbrella organization became greater.

Money orders sent to Greece by the Greeks in the United States reached $6,000,000.

1907   The largest number of Greeks in any one year, 36,580, arrived in the United States. This number equalled approximately 1.5 percent of the entire population of Greece at that time.

Greeks, wherever they settled, tended to form numerous organizations, often bitterly opposing one another. This isolated the Greek communities from their surroundings. There were about one hundred Greek organizations in the city of New York alone.

The Pan-Hellenic Union was founded in New York City.

The Greek consul general in New York City, Demetrios Botassi, wrote in his report to the Greek Foreign Ministry that "of the 150,000 Greeks in the U.S. between 30,-40,000 were working as laborers in factories and railraod construction gangs. Others were employed as bootblacks, waiters, and clerks in stores that catered to the immigrant trade."

Because of the economic depression in the United States, many Greeks returned to their homeland as they were among the first to be discriminated against. Adverse reports about Greek immigrants in America, describing the hard lot they were enduring, led the Greek government to advise provincial officers to discourage their citizens from emigrating. The reports by returning immigrants were often exaggerated, because they were reluctant to admit that they had been unable to succeed in America.

A Greek community began to form in Minneapolis, Minnesota.

The newspaper Ethniki was published in Boston, Mass.

The first Greek-American school was established in Boston. A secular school had also been founded in Lowell, at this time.

Workers from the Greek community in Lowell founded an acting group. The twenty members performed about ten modern Greek plays a year.

The Moraitis arrived in Piraeus. The ship was built especially to accommodate Greek emigrants and cargo, as it travelled from Piraeus to Kalamata and Patras, and then on to the United States.

Towards the latter part of the year Greeks renewed their exodus to the United States. By this time the financial and economic problems of the United States appeared to have been solved.

The Greeks had carried their factional strife with them to the new land. Although they settled immediately into communities and share the same problems, their intragroup differences did not diminish. Even the churches they established did not always help to create more harmonious communities. For this reason the Greeks began to form organizations. There were now approximately one hundred local societies (topika) formed by the Greeks in the United States, thirty of which were located in New York.

1908   The newspaper California began publication in San Francisco.

The first permanent Greek day school," Socrates ," was founded in Chicago. The school was sponsored by the Holy Trinity church.

A new trend in Greek immigration began. The Greek immigrants of the 1880s and 1890s had, for the most part, come from peasant stock. Now the educated class became convinced that they would more easily succeed than the peasants. Very often this group endured even greater hardships and had to take on menial jobs in order to exist. The biggest problem, as always, was the language barrier.

A Patriarchal Decree placed the Greek Orthodox Church of America under the Holy Synod of Greece.

1909   The cornerstone of the Greek Orthodox church of Tarpon Springs, Florida, was laid. The community was incorporated as the "Greek Orthodox Community of Tarpon Springs," and it was recognized as such by the state.

1909   The Temple of Theofokos was completed in Minneapolis, Minnesota. It was built in the Byzantine style. The first pastor ot that church was the Reverend Archimandrite Kyrillos Vapheiadakes.

A group of young Greeks formed the "Young Greeks' Progressive Society of Binghampton" in Alabama. It was founded as a mutual assistance society, and by 1910 it had 150 members.

Concerned by the news of riots and mob action against Greeks in Omaha, Nebraska, the Greek legation in Washington sent a letter of protest to the State Department and asked for protection and compensation for the Greeks who had lived in that city.

1910   The Greek community in Ely, Nevada, decided to form a company of volunteers and asked the Greek

consul in Chicago to help them find an instructor,
arms, and uniforms. Their action was mainly based on
the concern they felt for the problems Greece was
facing, which eventually led to the Balkan Wars in
1912 to 1913.

There were now fourteen Greek women to every one
hundred Greek men in the United States.

The headquarters of the Pan Hellenic Union was
moved to Boston. All local communities were placed
under its administration. The main objective of this
organization was to assist immigrants in adapting
to their new surroundings, while at the same time
teaching them about their heritage. Religion and the
Greek language were taught in schools established
by the Union.

The Koreas school was established in Chicago by
the community of Saints Constantine and Helen.

1911   The Greek Students Association Helicon was chartered
by thirteen students from Harvard, Tufts University,
and the Massachusetts Institute of Technology. It
was founded by Harvard student, B. Phoutrides. In
two years time, after communicating with Greek
students in other American colleges, Helicon had
forty members.

The newspaper Satyros was first published in New
York.

1912   At the outbreak of the Balkan Wars, the Greek government imposed restrictions on the emigration of Greek
males capable of fighting. The Pan Hellenic Union
took over the function of recruiting Greeks in the
United States to fight for Greece. It also raised
$375,000 to support the war. For these activities
the Pan Hellenic Union was severely criticized by
many Americans. It is estimated that between 30,-
40,000 Greek reservists and volunteers from all over
the United States left to aid Greece at this time.

During a strike at the mills in Lowell, Mass., Greek
workers, although striking with the rest, had to be
negotiated with separately. This action showed their

closeness in their community and their independence.

Because of the decline of production in the mills of Lowell, many Greeks began going West.

Constantine Papamichalopoulos, formerly a member of the Greek Parliament, came to the United States to become general manager of the Pan Hellenic Union.

At the annual meeting of the Pan Hellenic Union, 127 delegates and dignitaries voted affirmatively on the question of raising funds to assist Greeks in their fight against the Turks. They also decided to send aid to earthquake victims in the Aegean sea, to help establish the Greek Red Cross Society, and to support other worthwhile causes.

The Greek-American newspapers Light and Progress were first published in Salt Lake City, Utah. The Pan Hellenic Union established a branch in Salt Lake City.

The news that Henry Ford was paying five dollars a day in his automobile assembly line factories spread across the country. It brought many Greeks to Detroit who were seeking gainful employment.

1913 When the Balkan Wars ended, the flow of Greek immigrants to the United States increased and again reached its pre-war numbers.

The Hellenism Society, a benevolent association, was founded. At about the same time, natives from Krikoukios formed the Erythrai Society in Seattle, Washington.

It was reported that Birmingham, Alabama, had a Greek population of about 900.

The population of Tarpon Springs, Florida, numbered 4000. Approximately half of this community was Greek.

Six hundred Greeks were living in Washington, D.C., at this time.

Minneapolis, Minnesota, had a Greek community of about 500.

The Lowell community, the third largest colony of
Greeks in the United States, had 8000 parishioners.

The Greek population in the State of Washington,
centered mostly in Seattle, was between 6,-8,000.
Here, as in St. Louis, it increased greatly during
the winter months when railroad workers left their
temporary camps for the cities.

There were 4,000 Greeks living in Salt Lake City.
Here again the numbers might have varied because
of railroad workers passing through.

There were fifty-five Greek Orthodox churches in
the United States.

Chicago had over four hundred Greek confectionery
establishments, while New York had about one hundred
and fifty such stores and the same number of florists
owned by the Greeks.

The newspaper Atlantis had a circulation of 20,-
25,000. It was read all over the country and also in
Europe.

The newspaper Thessalonike was first published in
Chicago.

1914   Reverend S. Vaitis left Boston, where he was known
for his great devotion to the poor and sick, to continue his work in Lowell. In addition to his other
duties, he edited the religious monthly Aletheia
(Truth) and a newspaper, Angeliaforos (Messenger).

The Pan Hellenic Union invited Demetrios Callimachos
to come to the United States. He became a vociferous
spokesman for the Hellenic cause.

The Pan Hellenic Union had a paid membership of
almost five thousand. Its primary function was to re-
vitalize the Hellenic spirit in America.

The second largest number of Greek immigrants for
any one year, 35,832, arrived in the United States.

1915   The National Herald was first published in New York.

Petros Tatanis started the newspaper with a capital
investment of $100,000 in order to support the Veni-
zelos government in Greece. Demetrios Callimachos,
editor-in-chief of the daily, also became a leader
of the Venizelos movement in the United States. The
paper was thus started in opposition to the <u>Atlantis</u>,
published by Solon J. Vlasto, which expressed the
royalist sentiments in this country. Demetrios Callimachos did much to promote liberalism among Greek
immigrants, and his contribution to Greek-American
journalism was great.

Fifty thousand Greek immigrants came to the United
States between 1914 and 1915.

1916   October. Over three thousand Greeks met in New
York to form the Venizelos party in support of the provisional government of Eleutherios Venizelos in
Greece. A committee of one thousand was formed to
promote the party throughout the United States.

November. George Cafandaris and Panos Aravantinos
came to the United States to enlist Greeks and Americans for the national army in support of the Venizelos
government.

Branches of the Syndesmoi Nomotagon (Loyalist
Congress) began to appear in the major cities throughout America.

A number of the most influential Greeks in New York
formed the Hellenic Liberal Association. This was
an outgrowth of the October meeting in support of
Venizelos. The association was headed by Petros
Tatanis and Demetrios Callimachos.

Theoclitus, archbishop of Athens, proceeded to in-
flict the "medieval rite" on Venizelos. This led to
further conflicts and fights among Greeks in the United
States. Wherever Greeks met they were of opposing
factions. The American press and public were aghast
at their behaviour and as the conflict grew, the
sentiments against the Greek immigrants became
much stronger.

1917   January. Greek Americans appealed to President

Woodrow Wilson to prevent the blockade of Greece
by the allies.

February. Cafandaris and Aravantinos were invited by
the Greek Liberal Club of Chicago to speak at the
Coliseum Annex on behalf of Venizelos' Salonika
government. The Chicago Loyalty Leaguers, a group
of royalists, attempted to disrupt the rally. Although
some fighting did occur, and at least ten persons were
wounded and others arrested by the police, the rally
continued. It was estimated that some twelve thousand Greek-Americans attended the meeting.

April. Both the Venizelists and the royalists held
meetings and decided that they would support President Wilson and the United States in the war effort.

July. Two mass meetings were held in New York to
celebrate the return of Venizelos to Athens as prime
minister. The frictions and dissention in the Hellenic
Liberal Assocation led to the forming of a second
party, The League of Greek Liberals of New York,
which planned to have its own newspaper.

October. About one thousand anti-Venizelos Greeks
met at Carnegie Hall in New York City not to denounce
Venizelos but to support the cause of the allies.

November. The Relief Committee for Greeks in Asia
Minor held its first mass meeting at the Amsterdam
Opera House in New York. G. Roussos, the Greek
minister to the United States, addressed the audience.

The Literacy Law was imposed on all immigrants to the
United States. Until now immigration had been unre-
stricted. This new act was especially disastrous to
Greeks, since the majority of her emigrants came from
poor, uneducated, and illiterate peasant stock. The law
was enacted in 1918.

The Greek Minister of Foreign Affairs, Nicholas Politis, urged the Greek citizens in America to enlist in
the United States army. In a communique to George
Roussos, the Greek minister in Washington, he stated
that such enlistments would ". . .not entail the loss

of Greek nationality nor any other penalty against
the interested party, but on the contrary the Greek
government will recognize and reward all acts of
bravery performed by Greeks in the American army,
just as if these acts had been performed in the Greek
army."

Meletios Metaxakis became Metropolitan of Athens,
the titular head of the Church of Greece.

1918   May. The Greeks in the United States had purchased
approximately ten million dollars in liberty bonds.
This was looked upon favorably as an indication of
their dedication to this country.

July. A nationwide fund raising campaign was initiated
to aid the Greeks in Asia Minor and Thrace. Every
Greek American was asked to contribute a day's wages
in order to aid them in their struggle. Nicholas Kyriakides, the president of the Central Committee of
Unredeemed Greeks, the Greek Chamber of Commerce,
and Metropolitan Meletios Metaxakis gave strong
support to this campaign.

August. Metropolitan Metaxakis, primate of Greece,
visited America. During his visit he laid plans for
the organization and systematization of the Greek
Eastern Orthodox Church in America. The plan called
for an archbishop to be appointed to Washington,
D.C., and three bishops for New York, Chicago,
and Lowell or San Francisco. Meletios left Bishop
Alexander Rodostolou as the delegate of the Holy
Synod of Greece to supervise the Greek churches in
America.

Congress passed an act to authorize payment of in-
demnities to the government of Greece in settlement
of the claims for injuries caused to the Greek inhabitants of Omaha Nebraska in 1909. The sum awarded
was $40,000, while the Greek government had claimed
damages of $135,533.

There were now over one hundred Greek communities
in the United States. Manhattan, the borough of New
York City, alone had four such communities, which
had built churches. These Greek Orthodox churches

were located on East 72nd Street, West 54th Street,
West 24th Street, and Cedar Street.

George Dilboy became one of the first Greek American
war heroes during the First World War when he was
killed in action near Bellean Woods in France. He
was posthumously awarded the Congressional Medal
of Honor "for gallantry and intrepidity in action and
beyond the call of duty."

Twenty Greek newspapers were being published in
the United States.

Approximately one hundred and thirty Greek congregations had been formed by this date; sixty-one of
these since 1914.

Some 60,000 Greek-Americans had fought for the
United States in the First World War. By the end of
the war, Greeks had purchased Liberty Bonds in the
amount of $30,000,000 or more.

N. G. Kyriakides and C. Vassilakakis came to the
United States to inform the American people of the
atrocities being committed by the Turks and to gain
American support for their country, Greece.

The American Hellenic Society of New York was incorporated with the idea of strengthening the friendship between the citizens of America and Greece. Its
purpose was to promote economic, cultural, political,
social, and ethical relations between both countries;
to exchange students and to establish professorships
in the universities of America and Greece.

1919   February. Representatives of Armenians, Greeks, and
Jews, who had been subjected to Turkish rule, held a
meeting in New York City. These groups agreed to aid
each other to achieve their respective national aspirations.

April. Momotagis (The Loyalist) was first published
in New York. It began as a weekly to support the Royalists in their anti-Venizelos campaign.

May. The Loyalty League of New York sponsored a

rally to dramatize the patriotism of the Greek-American community. This was just one of many attempts by various Greek organizations to demonstrate to the American people the progress they had made in their movement toward Americanization.

There was a great deal of political unrest among and within the Greek-American communities. The political problems of the mother country were taken up and vigorously supported by the Greek immigrants and their descendants. Many of their conflicts were due to the bitter opposition of Royalists versus Venizelists.

The Pan-Epirotic Union had twenty-six chapters in America. The main purpose of this organization was to work for the unification of all northern Epirus with Greece.

The American Hellenic National Union was established in Massachusetts. Its purpose was "to assist those who have selected America as their home learning the English language, and in understanding the guiding laws of the United States."

1921   April. Archbishop Meletios came to America to support the appointment of Alexander Rodostolou as the first archbishop of the Greek Orthodox Church in America.

June. Germanos Trojanos, bishop of Sparta and Monemvasia, arrived in New York. He had been appointed by the Synod as synodical exarch in North and South America. The Greek priests and communities were divided in their support of Rodostolou and Trojanos for bishop.

September. Meletios Metaxakis incorporated the Greek Archdiocese of North and South America under the Religious Corporation Law of New York State.

The first American edition of Ekklesiastikos Kyrix (Church Herald) was published.

October. D. J. Theophialotos, stating that he spoke for 105 Greek organizations in the United States, sent the following telegram to ex-King Constantine at Luzerne, Switzerland: "American Greeks strongly oppose

any concessions to any foreign influences calculated
to deprive the Greek people of their inalienable rights
to demand your Majesty's return to the throne of
Greece, which by inheritance and tradition belongs
to you."

The Seminary of St. Athanasius was established under
the direction of Meletios Metaxakis. It was hoped
that the seminary would prepare young men for the
priesthood in America. Its first director was Archimandrite Philaretos.

Eleutherios Venizelos, the former prime minister of
Greece, visited the United States. He sailed from
London to New York, where he spent a few days before heading west to Santa Barbara, California, where
he planned to spend the winter. In Chicago, an estimated ten thousand people crowded into La Salle Street
Station in order to catch a glimpse of Venizelos and
the Metropolitan of Athens when they arrived. After
being escorted through the waiting throngs, the two
men proceeded to their hotel where it was said twenty
thousand admirers had gathered, shouting "Venizelos
our hero! Long live Venizelos our saint!"

November. The first Greek Theological Seminary was
inaugurated by Meletios Metaxakis in the auditorium
of the 23rd Street Y.M.C.A. in New York City. There
were only six students in the first class.

December. Metaxakis, the ecumenical patriarch, met
with President Warren G. Harding.

December. A special service was held in honor of
Metaxakis at the church of St. John the Devine. Dignitaries from other religious groups attended the ceremony, including representatives of the Episcopalian,
the Russian, the Armenian and the Syrian churches.

According to a bulletin issued by the Bank of Greece,
$114,010,259 was received through immigrant remit-
tances. Most of this amount was reported to have
come from Greeks living in the United States.

The United States Census reported that 175,972
foreign born Greeks were living in the United States.

Adding to this number another twenty percent for
children of these born here, resulted in 211,666
Greek people classified by the Census as "Foreign"
white stock. Of these 38,574 were living in New
England, and 24,122 in Massachusetts alone.

A Greek, by the name of Trivoulides, won the Marathon race in Boston, Massachusetts.

The number of Greek women in the United States had
increased to twenty-three to every one hundred Greek-
American men.

Greek organizations and "Friends of Greece" spent
much of the year lobbying in the United States Senate,
in order to gain support for Greek territorial claims.

The Quota System for European countries was established, limiting the number of immigrants from one
country in any one year to three percent of the number
of their natives living in the United States in 1910.
This new restriction on immigration was a further
blow to Greeks who had just begun to come to this
country in substantial numbers.

When Venizelos had said at the Versailles Peace
Conference, "A Greek is a person who wants to be
a Greek, feels he is a Greek and says he is a Greek,"
he was very much describing the Greeks in the United
States. Although making many efforts to become
Americanized, the majority of them still felt primarily Greek, and most of their actions were aimed toward
assisting their country of origin.

FROM HELLENISM TO AMERICANIZATION
1920s - 1940s

The post World War I era saw a change in attitude in Greek-American communities throughout the United States. Nationalistic ties to the mother country were weakened. The traditionalist viewpoint was losing ground as Greeks in America became more concerned with American issues.

The defeat of the Greeks in Asia Minor in 1922 forced the Greeks in America to realize that their influence on both the Greek and American governments was severely limited. In addition, having been defrauded of their savings by the financial institutions of their birthplace, Greek-American faith in the Greek banking system dwindled. That loss of faith compounded the gradual withdrawal of their concern for the affairs of Greece. The Greek immigrant was no longer here just to save enough money to pay off the mortgage on the paternal property and then return to Greece. Now, committed to the United States, he was here to stay and wanted to adapt to his new homeland.

1922   January. The State Department received an urgent message from Rear-Admiral Mark S. Bristol, the United States high commissioner in Constantinople recounting a plot to assassinate Venizelos in the United States. As there had been several similar rumors of Turkish plots, he discounted the story.

January. President Harding received telegrams from royalist groups in various parts of the country. Notably represented were: New York, Boston, Akron, Springfield, Norfolk, Salem, Nashville, Pittsfield, Burlington, Hartford, and Lexington, Kentucky. These petitions called for a resumption of closer official relations between the United States and Greece.

February. Meletios Metaxakis was officially enthroned as Ecumenical Patriarch. Although he only reigned for less than a year, he helped to revoke the Decree of 1908 restoring jurisdiction over the United States churches to the Ecumenical Patriarchate, and under his leadership, the Archdiocese of North and South America was established. One of his first official decrees on March 1, was to revoke the dependence of Greek Orthodoxy in America on the Holy Synod of Greece. This was formalized on May 11 when Patriarch Meletios declared the Church of America an Archdiocese, appointing the Right Reverend Alexander, Titular Bishop of Rodostolou, to be his Patriarchal Exarch in America.

May. Venizelos sailed for Europe. His trip to the United States had been successful for he was received enthusiastically by the Greek communities in those cities where he stopped. He also met with President Harding and with Secretary of State Hughes.

May. The National Herald tried to establish an organized union of Greek-Americans by sponsoring a national defense fund for Greece.

August. The second assembly of clergy and laymen was called into session by Bishop Alexander. The participants at the assembly drafted a constitution for the archdiocese which provided for bishops in New York City, Chicago, Boston, and San Francisco.

September. The seventeenth of this month was selected by the Greek churches in Chicago, Philadelphia, New York City and other metropolitan areas as the Sunday that all the faithful should attend church and pray for the salvation of Greece.

September. George A. Nicholopoulos and John (Ionnis) Angelopoulos formed AHEPA (the American Hellenic Educational Progressive Association) in Atlanta, Georgia. The State of Georgia recognized the organization on September 25. On the same date, AHEPA, legally incorporated, was given a twenty year charter. AHEPA's aim was to unite Greeks and build a stronger front against anti-Greek sentiments that were spreading throughout the United States, and which became pervasive after the war. The primary function of AHEPA was "to advance and promote pure and undefiled Americanism among the Greeks of the United States, its Territories and Colonial possessions; to educate the Greeks in the matter of democracy, and

government of the United States, and for the general
promotion of fraternity, sociability and the practice
of benevolent aid among this nationality."

September. The news that King Constantine had abdi-
cated was very well received by the Greek-American
liberals. In fact, the National Herald ran a front page
headline proclaiming: "The Traitor Falls".

December. Members of the Holy Trinity Church of
Lowell, Massachusetts, the center of Greek royalism
in the United States were planning the development
of an autocephalous church. This direction, toward
a schism, was considered antithetical to the aims of
the Ecumenical Patriarchate and the Church of Greece.
Thus, when their spiritual leader, Germanos, returned
to Greece and their schism was declared illegal, the
presidency was restored to an adherent of canonical
law who brought the Holy Trinity back into the fold.

At the end of the First World War Greece was forced
to provide shelter for almost one and a half million
refugees from Turkey. Greece was unable to sustain
the burden; fortunately emigration brought some
relief.

The State of New York recognized the Greek Orthodox
Church. The Reverend Alexander was appointed its
first archbishop.

The Union of Macedonian Political Organizations was
founded in Indiana. It later changed its name, in
1952, to the Macedonian Patriotic Organization of
the United States and Canada. The organization was
formed to preserve the Macedonian culture and heritage and to unite its members in social and cultural
activities.

During the course of this year 28,502 Greek immigrants
arrived in the United States. It was the third largest
annual influx since the defeat of Greece by Turkey.

1923   January. Bishop Germanos formally announced the
              termination of his exarchal role.

              May. Democratic Liberals in the United States and

Canada held a convention in Chicago on May 11 and
12. The primary purpose of the meeting was to en-
sure the election of the democratic candidates in
Greece.

June. Archmandrite Philaretos was chosen bishop of
Chicago and was consecrated as such in St. Constantine's church in a ritualistic ceremony lasting three
hours.

June. Archmandrite Joachim was chosen bishop of
Boston.

October. There were thirty-two chapters of AHEPA in
existence at this time, the date of its first national
convention.

October. The editorship of Ekklesiastikos Kyrix was
taken up by Michael Galanos.

December. The Greek American Progressive Association (GAPA) was formed. For the most part, it was
created to counteract the ideals proposed by AHEPA.
In contrast to AHEPA, GAPA held that Americanization
would necessarily weaken the Greek heritage because
it would lead to the demise of the Greek language,
church and traditions in the United States. GAPA was
founded, therefore, to promote the Greek language,
support the Orthodox Church, and to generally oppose
the ideals of AHEPA.

Greek-Americans were urged to take an active role in
furthering the democratic movement in Greece. To
this end, Thalis Koutoupis, a feature writer for the
National Herald in Athens; Speros Kotakis, editor of
Kathemerini in Chicago; and Andrew Vlachos, a
prominent lawyer in Chicago attempted to promote the
Panhellenic ideal among Greek-Americans. It was
their hope that the Greek nation would grant the Greek-
Americans representation in the Greek Chamber of
Deputies.

The Metropolitan of Chaldea, Vasileos Komvopoulos,
arrived in the United States. He intended to take up
where Bishop Germanos had left off. After a few
months of campaigning he declared himself "the

Autocephalous Head of the Greek Churches in the
United States and Canada."

The Empros (Forward) was first published and remained
the mouthpiece of Greek-speaking Communists for
sixteen years.

1924   January. The United States resumed its diplomatic
relations with Greece.

May. The Holy Synod in Constantinople instructed
Archbishop Alexander to publicize its decree, reducing
Vasileos to "the ranks of the laity" in one Greek and
one American newspaper. This had the effect of not
degrading Vasileos but of elevating him to the position
of martyr.

The Johnson-Reed Act was adopted, limiting the number
of immigrants from each country to two percent of those
born in that country and living in the United States in
1890. This rule further restricted the number of Greeks
who would be permitted to come to America. Only
307 Greeks were allowed to enter as immigrants per
year. The Greeks denounced both the 1921 Emergency
Quota Act and the 1924 Johnson-Reed Act as discriminatory.

1925   The Hellenic Professional Society of Illinois was
established.

The National League of Greek Voters (NLGV) was
organized by political activists who sought support
from Republican leaders in return for their support
during all presidential and important state elections.
But this attempt to set up a country-wide union failed.
Meanwhile, local political clubs seemed to grow in
strength and number.

1926   January. The Sons of Pericles organization was
founded in Manchester, New Hampshire. Once established, it became a junior order of AHEPA and aimed
to promote the Americanization of second generation
Greeks.

1927   June. The New York Times reported that measures for
the reorganization of the Greek Church in America were

decided upon by the minister of education in Athens.
The Greek Church in America was described as in a
state of disorganization. The ministry announced that
it would be revived under the Church of Greece, which
would send clergymen "to replace irregularly appointed
bishops."

1928   Representatives of the Greek Orthodox Church and
         Greek government were planning to build a Greek
         village near Wantagh, Long Island, containing a
         church and a university. The village was to be called
         "New Athens" and the university the "Hellenic Insti-
         tute of Learning."

         Damaskinos, the Metropolitan of Corinth arrived in the
         United States to collect donations for victims of the
         Corinth earthquake.

         A delegation from the Alfred E. Smith for President
         Greek-American Political Club met with presidential
         candidate Smith at the Congress Hotel in Chicago.

         At their national convention, members of AHEPA voted
         to exclude all members of GAPA from being eligible
         for membership in its organization.

1929   In order to unite women of Greek descent, the Daugh-
         ters of Penelope was founded. By 1975, this organ-
         ization had a membership of about 13,000.

         The Pancretan Association of America was founded in
         California. It is a fraternal organization which pro-
         duces a monthly publication entitled Crete .

         The Pan-Rhodian Society of America, Apollon Inc.,
         was founded in Virginia. The society is primarily for
         for those Greeks and their descendants who have
         emigrated to the United States from the Rhodes area.
         Since 1930 it has sponsored the monthly publication
         of Apollon.

1930   April. The Ecumenical Patriarchate appointed Damas-
         kinos to be Patriarchal Exarch of the United States.
         This was an attempt to unify the church and to bring
         peace to the conflicting factions.

May. Damaskinos arrived in the United States on his mission of peace. A short while after his arrival, he left for Washington, D.C. to meet with President Hoover. Upon his return to New York he delved into the task at hand.

May. Damaskinos sent his first encyclical letter and copies of three other letters to the heads of the church communities. The enclosures consisted of: a letter from the Patriarch which introduced the Exarch and his mission; an admonishing letter to the Greek-Americans from the Patriarch, telling them that it was time to forget their differences and unite; and a letter from the Metropolitan of Athens, telling the Americans of Greek descent to assist the Exarch in his work wherever possible.

June. Across the United States, Greek organizations, societies, clubs and church communities were meeting to decide upon Damaskinos's encyclical. Overwhelmingly, the communities chose to uphold the Exarch and to support his efforts toward unity. As a result, the synodical system was abolished by the Ecumenical Patriarchate, and the Archdiocese as we know it today was established.

June. Archbishop Alexander, who had vehemently opposed the Exarch, was dismissed without trial and stripped of all his authority. He was not alone in his opposition to Damaskinos. The Atlantis of New York and the Hellinikos Astir of Chicago both protested the methods of the Exarch.

August. Athenagoras, the Metropolitan of Corfu, became the archbishop of North and South America after being recommended by Damaskinos as a suitable replacement for Alexander.

The proportion of Greek women to Greek men in the United States had by this time considerably improved. There were now thirty-five women to every 100 men. A total of 303,751 Greeks were residing in the United States according to the United States Department of the Census, of which 129,225 were second generation.

Over the previous two decades, 250,000 people, most

of them refugees, emigrated from Greece a significant proportion of whom were from Turkey. In the
wake of the Balkan Wars and the First World War,
and especially after the tragic defeat in Asia Minor,
almost one million had fled to Greece mostly from
Turkey. Many of these refugees then made their way
to the United States for Greece could not support this
crippling burden.

1931   February. Archbishop Athenagoras arrived in New York,
            thereby beginning a long tenure as the head of the
            Greek Orthodox Church in America, which continued
            until he was elected Ecumenical Patriarch of Constan-
            tinople on November 1, 1948. A remarkable ecclesiast
            with great dedication, energy and charismatic person-
            ality, Archbishop Athenagoras initiated an authoritative
            administration that went far towards uniting the Greek
            communities in America under a centralized archdiocese,
            and laid a sure groundwork for the future of Greek
            Orthodoxy in the United States. In addition to his
            good work for American communicants, before he
            assumed the spiritual leadership of the world's 150
            million Greek Orthodox believers as Ecumenical
            Patriarch, Athenagoras attained a high degree of influ-
            ence among Americans, who respected and admired him.

            April. The United States Department of State was
            informed that the Greek government had continued for
            the past year the policy adopted in 1929, whereby
            American citizens of Greek extraction who held American
            passports could visit Greece for three months without
            being required to perform military service. This exemp-
            tion applied to persons born in the United States of
            Greek parents and to Greeks who had been naturalized
            as citizens of the United States.

            Philoptochos, the Greek Orthodox Ladies Philanthropic
            Organization was established. Its purpose was "to
            fulfill all the philanthropic, charitable and elemosynary
            objectives of the Church, which include aid to those
            in need of guidance and referral in every community,
            as regards to public services, old age assistance,
            scholastic and educational institutions, as well as
            those in need of emergency financial assistance."

            In Chicago, the Greek-language newspapers Democrat,

Salonike, Kathemerini and Hellinikos Astir united
their efforts in support of mayorial candidate A. J.
Cermak. This was illustrative of a trend, whereby
Greek-Americans would shy away from the Republican
Party in favor of Democratic Party ideals and candi-
dates.

According to the Annual Report of the Commissioner
General of Immigration, as of the end of the fiscal
year, 197,088 Greeks had returned to their homeland
between 1908 and 1931. This was a significant proportion of the roughly 500,000 Greek immigrants who
had come to the United States. Compared to other
ethnic groups, Greeks were fourth in the percentage
of immigrants returning home.

1932   More than one hundred leading Greek industrialists,
exporters, importers and bankers met in New York
City to discuss the establishment of better trade
relations between the United States and Greece. The
program finally adopted called for the formation of a
Greek Chamber of Commerce.

1933   The depression had pronounced effects upon the
church communities. Bishop Kallistos of Chicago
announced that all of the churches in his district had
been unable to raise the money necessary to cover
their operating costs during the fiscal year.

1935   July. Former Prime Minister Alexander Papanastasiou
arrived in the United States. The purpose of his visit
was to ask the Greek-American community to support
national unity in Greece so as to rid that country of
its political unrest. To his mind this end would best
be served by the perpetuation of the republic.

August. The director of the Greek Secret Service ,
Colonel Zezas reported to the War Minister, George
Kondylis, that a large quantity of money had been
gathered by Alexander Papanastasiou. These funds
were collected from Greeks in the United States to
support the republican movement and to finance the
republican campaign during the plebiscite on monarch-
ial restoration. He also reported that one million
drachmas had been sent by Venizelos, former premier,
and his son to support the labor movement and to

strengthen the anti-monarchist front.

August. The president of the Greco-American Delphic
Society sent War Minister Kondylis a telegram pledging its members' readiness to support restoration.

August. Greek-Americans belonging to twelve chapters
of the National Union in Chicago cabled Premier
Panayoti Tsaldaris and declared themselves supporters
of restoration. They condemned the "Communist and
Republican" campaign of former Premier Papanastasiou
in the United States.

August. Greek-Americans in the New England states
sent a telegram to War Minister Kondylis to ask the
governent to sustain "normal democratic government."

October. Dr. Cleanthes Vassardakis, former Greek
consul general in San Francisco and head of the
Hellenic National League in the United States sent a
cablegram to Premier Tsaldaris which urged that King
George be called back to the throne without a plebiscite.

1936   John Metaxas became the leader of Greece and conver-
            ted the government into a dictatorship. A concerted
            effort was made by various members of the Greek-
            language press, business and professional men,
            clergymen and dignitaries to convince the Greek-
            Americans of the merits of the new regime.

            The Maids of Athens was established as an organi-
            zation for females of Greek descent which aimed
            at preserving Greek traditions and values in the United
            States. Within forty years there would be 155 branches
            of this organization located in cities throughout the
            United States.

            Dimitri Mitropoulos, the conductor, came to the United
            States.

1937   The National Greek-American Patriotic Committee
            planned to sponsor the publication of The Greek Blue
            Book listing names and addresses of more than 55,000
            Greek-American merchants throughout the United States.
            It was reported that Greek-Americans operated more
            than 70,000 retail stores in the United States and

that Greek-American merchants purchased more
than $750,000,000 worth of merchandise annually.
Also, 40,325 or 26.9 per cent of the restaurants in
the country and 10,024 or 18.1 per cent of the candy
and confectionery stores were operated by Greek-
Americans.

At a meeting of the Greek Union for Democracy, Dr.
Peter Kekes, a physician, charged the Metaxas regime
with spreading pro-fascist propaganda authorized by
Demetrios Sicilianos, Greek minister to the United
States, and filtered through Greek consuls general in
American cities. He also accused the Greek Orthodox
Church, the local Greek press and businessmen of
negative support of the government in power to insure
the safety of their interests abroad.

Archbishop Athenagoras I established the Holy Cross
Theological school in Pomfret Center, Connecticut.
Without funds, but with great faith and determination
he built the foundations of the seminary assisted by
the New England parishes. Classes began on October
3, with three teachers and fourteen students. The
original intent of the founder and the first dean was
that Holy Cross would serve as a two-year prepara-
tory school whose graduates would complete their
training for the priesthood at the Theological School
of the University of Athens, Greece, or at the Theological School of Halki in Constantinople (Istanbul).
However, these plans were frustrated by World War
II. Not only did it become impossible to send students
to Europe for theological training, but it also became
impossible to bring priests from Greece and Turkey as
had been the practice. Thus, the original plans for
the school had to be revised so that the students would
have the opportunity to complete their training without
having to go abroad. The curriculum was extended to
five years and patterned along the academic traditions
of the Orthodox theological schools of Europe.

Professor Vasilios G. Valaoras stated in The Hellenism
of the United States that the steady flow of money from
the Greek immigrants in America had helped solve
Greece's economic problems. From 1814 onwards money
had been transferred to Greece regularly from these
sources but, naturally, the flow had slowed down

during the Depression.

The Greek-American Union for Democracy was organized. As a communist front group, it lead a spirited fight against fascism.

1938   During their national convention, the members of AHEPA discussed the dangers of fascism, communism and anti-Semitism, and passed resolutions endorsing democracy and individual liberties.

Chicago had the largest Greek population of any American city. There were approximately sixty thousand "Chicagopolites" as they called themselves, living in "Chicagopolis."

Nikos Moshonas, the baritone, arrived in the United States.

1939   The Metaxas government sought with greater fervor to gain the support of the Greeks in America. With this end in view, Metaxas sent his chief propagandist, Vasileos Papadakis to the United States. When he arrived in New York he was met by the Greek consul general, the editor-in-chief of Atlantis, and a representative of Archbishop Athenagoras.

The Eleutheria (Liberty) became the organ of Greek-American Communists and continued as such until April 1941 when its publication was terminated.

Alika, the well-known Greek actress, arrived in the United States.

1940   July. One thousand representatives of Greek-American societies celebrated America's Independence Day with services at the Greek Cathedral, 319 East Seventy-fourth Street, New York City, under the auspices of the Federation of Greek Societies of Greater New York. Archbishop Athenagoras officiated.

August. The First Pan-Hellenic Congress met in Cincinnati, attended by 461 delegates of Greek clubs and organizations throughout the United States. It was officially opened by Sam Rayburn, the speaker of the House of Representatives, who gave a speech and delivered a statement for President Roosevelt.

October. According to State Department records, there were about 4,500 United States citizens in Greece at this time, most of them Greeks who, after obtaining American citizenship, returned to their home country.

The Greek War Relief Association (GWPA) was founded under the direction of Spyros Skouras, less than a fortnight after Greece was invaded. In its first news release, GWPA reported that the activities of approximately two thousand Greek organizations, clubs and societies had been organized so that they could be coordinated by about three hundred local committees. Although many of the Greek-American groups helped in this endeavor, AHEPA was by far the most supportive organization.

Athene, one of the most popular Greek-American magazines, was first published in Chicago by D. Michalaros. It continued publication for over twenty-five years.

1941   September. Spyros Skouras, the head of the GWRA in the United States, reported that plans had been completed for food purchased in Turkey to be shipped to Greece. He denied that only the wealthy would be aided by this venture.

October. Archbishop Athenagoras performed the holy rites of elevation and raised Archimandrite Eirinaois Tsourounakis of the Church of the Annunciation, New York, to the office of bishop of San Francisco.

The Reverend Dr. Germanos Polizoides, rector of St. Demetrios Hellenic Orthodox church in New York, was elevated to the post of bishop of Chicago, the second most important office in the Church in the Americas. Archbishop Athenagoras made this announcement after he had received instructions from Patriarch Benjamin of the Church of Constantinople. The position had been vacant for about a year, since the death of Bishop Callistos.

A few months after its inception, GWRA reported that approximately 964 chapters had been founded and that more than $5,250,000 had been collected.

1942   AHEPA began a campaign to sell $50 million worth of
        liberty bonds. The drive kicked off with a broadcast
        of speeches made by Sam Rayburn, the speaker of the
        House, and George C. Vournas, the president of
        AHEPA.

        The Pan-Hellenic Federation was established. Its
        primary purpose was to coordinate the activities of
        all Greek-American organizations.

        The Panepirotic Federation was formed under the aegis
        of Archbishop Athenagoras, to aid Greece in obtaining
        her territorial claims.

        A statue of the Greek-American hero, G. Dilboy, was
        unveiled in Hines, Illinois, by George C. Vournas.

1943   February. Dr. Stephen Ladas, secretary of the Friends
        of Greece, announced that an initial gift of $500 had
        been donated to finance plans for the reconstruction
        of Greek cities and towns destroyed or damaged by
        the Axis powers. The plans were to be drawn up at
        Columbia University's School of Architecture.

        February. Representatives of the United Greek Ortho-
        dox Churches in the Americas presented President
        Roosevelt with the Grand Cross of the Holy Sepulchre.
        It is the highest blessing the Greek church can bestow
        and was given to the president in acknowledgement
        of his "nobility of mind and heart, in appreciation of
        [his] ceaseless efforts in behalf of liberty, justice
        and peace and in recognition of the fact that the es-
        sence of Christ's teachings is found in the four free-
        doms of the Atlantic Charter."

        August. The Eastern Orthodox congregations united
        to celebrate the mass of St. John Chrysostum and to
        mark the beginning of the federation of the Church.
        Prayers were offered in Greek, Arabic, English, and
        Slavonic. The Federation of the Orthodox Churches
        in America was organized to gather the Orthodox
        people into one fellowship.

        President Roosevelt and the Greek Ambassador to the

United States, Cimon P. Diamantopoulous, spoke at ceremonies marking the transfer of a 173-foot submarine chaser, renamed the King George II, to the government of Greece.

The archdiocese inaugurated its monodollarion program, a voluntary per capita annual contribution of one dollar. This greatly increased the Church's revenues but was not as easy to impliment as it seemed. The growth in revenues collected from 1942 to 1944 was over twenty thousand dollars: $41,000 was collected in 1942 and $62,500 in 1944.

1944   March. Vice President Wallace spoke in Boston in celebration of the 123rd anniversary of Greek Independence Day. He said that the United States was pledged to fight until the people of Greece and other nations were free. Other speakers included: Representative John W. McCormack; Mayor Tobin; Cimon P. Diamantopoulous; and Charles A. Maliotis, president of the Federation of Greek Communities and Societies of Greater Boston.

September. The House of Hellas, the new headquarters of the Friends of Greece, Inc., was opened to the public, as was announced by the organization's president, Mrs. William Astor Chanler. The organization conducted sales of merchandise for funds to carry on the work of shipping food, medicine and clothing to Greek war victims.

October. In a letter to Basil J. Vlavianos, the editor of the National Herald, President Roosevelt declared: "America has always had the highest regard for the gallant Greek people who gave birth to democracy. ...I am glad to have this opportunity to reassure my friends of Greek origin and Greek birth everywhere that it is the desire of the American government to help Greece to the utmost of its capabilities."

October/November. Approximately 25,000 Greek-Americans rallied in New York to celebrate the fourth anniversary of Greece's defense against Mussolini and to celebrate the landing of the Allied forces in Greece. The Greek ambassador to the United States, speaking at the rally, advised Greeks in America to forget their political differences and unite so as to help rebuild their mother country.

November. Dr. Michael Mandelenakis, the secretary of the Greek-American Committee for National Unity reported that many of the news releases from Greece were "false propaganda emanating from reactionary sources. " His reaction against criticisms of the National Liberation Front (EAM) led him to state that: "The overwhelming majority of the Greek people who support the EAM, far from seeking civil war, are displaying the highest discipline and order."

The Academy of St. Basil's was founded in Garrison, New York. The objectives of this institution were defined from the beginning as the development of education, as characterized by the Greek Orthodox tradition, and the practice of charity. In accordance with these objectives, two departments were established within its grounds: (1) The Teachers Training Department for training teachers and secretaries for the Greek communities in this country; and (2) The Children's Home, to provide shelter and education to needy children of Greek descent, orphans, and children from broken homes. In addition, St. Basil's provided a summer camp program for children of the First Diocese and housed a convent.

Loucas Kyrides received an award from the American Chemical Association for "over one hundred inventions and contributions to the field of chemistry."

The Taylor Scholarship Foundation was established by S. Gregory Taylor to provide financial assistance to theology graduates of Holy Cross Seminary.

1945   February. The Greek-American Council (GAC) was established in New York City. The Greek-American Labor Committee and the Greek-American Committee for National Unity (GACFNU) were both forerunners of the GAC. The change in name, however, did not result in a change in policy.

June. Upon his return to the United States from a two-month visit to Greece, Spyros Skouras announced that 1,400 Greek villages had been burned. He estimated

that approximately 500,000 Greeks were homeless
and in need of aid.

November. The supreme president of the American
Hellenic Educational Progressive Association asserted
that all Greek-Americans would adamantly protest the
financial and territorial arrangements between Greece
and Bulgaria which were said to have been approved
by Secretary of State James F. Byrnes.

The Greek War Relief Association reported that between
1942 and 1945, it sent nine million dollars in supplies
and money to Greece, donated by Americans as well
as Greek organizations all over the United States.

Between 1921 and 1945, 432,000 Greeks emigrated
from Greece proper, another 156,000 came from the
European part of Turkey, and 205,474 arrived from
Asia Minor.

The Greek language newspaper _Ethnikos Frouros_ was
first published in Chicago, and the _Life of Greece_
began publication in Boston.

1946   AHEPA welcomed the first American president into its
            ranks when President Harry S. Truman became a mem-
            ber. Although Franklin D. Roosevelt was a member
            of AHEPA, he became so when he was governor of
            New York.

            The Greeks of Tarpon Springs, Florida, who had come
            chiefly from the Dodecanese Islands, succeeded in
            having these Mediterranean islands returned to
            Greece. The United States Senate Committee on
            Foreign Relations unanimously adapted a resolution
            proposed by Senator Claude Pepper of Florida that the
            Dodecanese Islands and northern Epiras should be
            awarded to Greece. This was a significant victory
            for the Greek-American organizations which had applied
            efforts in support of this cause, such as: the Panhellen-
            ic Committee for the Defense of Greek Rights, the
            National Justice for Greece Committee, the American
            Justice for Greece Committee, and the Panepirotic
            Federation as well as AHEPA and GAPA.

            Under the leadership of George P. Skouras, GWRA

initiated a "Give an Animal" campaign. Greek agriculture was in grave need of rehabilitation. Greek-Americans were convinced of this need and contributed funds to help restock depleted farm animals.

Representatives of the Ethnikon Apelentheritikon Metopon (EAM) or the National Liberation Front of Greece toured the United States for two months. The delegation was led by G. Georgalas, a professor of mineralogy at the University of Athens before the Nazi invasion, a member of the Socialist Party on the central committee of the EAM, and the president of the Greek Youth Movement, together with Nicholas Carvounis, the press director of the EAM in Athens. After speaking to various groups around the country they returned to Greece. But shortly before they departed the American Relief for Greek Democracy was established to supply aid to the EAM forces.

AHEPA first concentrated its war relief effort on hospital programs. Five months after the inception of a nation-wide drive it had already raised one million dollars.

ERA OF PHILHELLENISM
1940s to the Present

The Second World War had profound effects upon
Greek communities in the United States. No
longer were they looked upon suspiciously or
considered undesirable aliens by the American
people. After the heroic resistance staged by
Greece against Mussolini's invading forces,
all Greeks were filled with a new sense of pride.
Americans of Greek descent shared this pride,
and now not only declared that they were proud
to be American but also once again loudly proclaimed that they were proud to be Greek.

The Greeks in America, never altogether indif-
ferent to the plight of their mother country, now
exhibited signs of a reawakening concern. This
surge of Philhellenism manifested itself in many
ways. During the war, Greek-Americans banded
together to aid Greece through the GWRA and
AHEPA. In the aftermath of the war, these Greeks
were instrumental in influencing the United States
government to favor Greece, as is reflected in
the Truman Doctrine and again in the Marshall
Plan. Today, the Americans of Greek descent
have their own representatives in Washington,D.C.
Their lobbyists act on the basis of the support
and concern of Greeks in the United States for
their mother country and argue the views of Greek-
Americans on the Cyprus issue.

Throughout this period of Philhellenism, the ties
between the Greeks in America and the Greeks in
Greece grew stronger. Greek-Americans have
wanted to establish a closer contact with their
heritage and many in recent years have crossed the
Atlantic to visit their mother country.

1947   March. On the occasion of the eleventh anniversary
              of the death of Venizelos, Archbishop Athenagoras
              gave praise to President Truman and announced that
              the 300 churches under his leadership would be offer-

ing prayers for the president's continued good health.

The Pan-Macedonian Association was founded in New York for people in the United States and Canada who emigrated from Macedonia, and for their descendants. Its main purpose is to promote Greek - United States relations, disseminate information about Macedonia, and send aid to that region. Since 1953, the Pan-Macedonian Association has published the bimonthly Macedonia in Greek and English.

1948   Archbishop Athenagoras was chosen as Ecumenical Patriarch, thus becoming the first American citizen to reach the supreme throne of the Orthodox Church. When he departed the United States for Istanbul, he traveled in the private plane of the president of the United States.

The Daughters of Evrythania was established in Charlotte, North Carolina. It is primarily a charitable organization whose main purpose is to aid the province of Evrytania in Greece.

1949   Archbishop Michael, who succeeded Patriarch Athenagoras as Archbishop of North and South America, retained the appointment until his death on July 13, 1958. As a leader, he most effectively furthered the consolidating work of his illustrious predecessor and thereby greatly strengthened the Greek Orthodox Church in America. During this period, with its added resources and activities, the Church can be seen to have been entering a stage of maturity. Among Archbishop Michael's many accomplishments was the founding of the Greek Orthodox Youth in America (GOYA) and the forming of the first Greek Orthodox Home for the Aged in Yonkers, New York.

1950   The report on international migration and naturalization of the Bureau of the Census showed a decrease in the number of foreign-born Greeks living in America. The number reported was 169,335.

The first Greek Orthodox church to be built in the United States, Holy Trinity in New Orleans, was demolished. A new church was erected on the site where the old one had stood.

At the Tenth Biennial Congress of Clergymen and Laymen a compulsory dekadollarion was authorized. Now,
a ten dollar per capita annual contribution to the
church was made mandatory, superseding the voluntary
one dollar contribution declaration of 1943. The
Archdiocese revenues increased greatly, from about
$82,000 in 1950 to nearly $330,000 in 1951. By 1955
contributions topped the half million dollar mark.

1951   The Greek Orthodox Youth of America was founded.
The main purpose of this organization is to provide
activities that develop the Greek Orthodox faith,
to promote the Greek heritage in America, and to
allow social and athletic development among the
Greek youth. In 1965 it began the monthly publication,
Challenge, and in 1970 also sponsored the monthly
publication of Be Ye Advised. By the mid-1970s,
GOYA had a membership numbering approximately 200,000.

1952   The McGarran-Walter Act set the quota for Greek immigrants at 308 per year. It did however, make some
provisions for refugees and displaced persons, increasing the number on that basis to between 2,000
and 3,000 Greeks annually.

1954   The Board of Collegiate Authorities of the State of
Massachusetts granted to Holy Cross the right to con-
fer upon its graduates the degree of Bachelor of Arts
in Theology. In 1956, the same Board of Collegiate
Authorities bestowed upon the school the right to con-
fer the degree of Bachelor of Divinity (B.D.) and also
the degree of Master of Sacred Theology (S.T.M.).

Constantine Zambounis, the editor and publisher of
the satyrical weekly Satyros since its inception in
1911, died. His devastating satire in verse, prose
and cartoons reflected and interpreted the problems
of the Greek immigrant.

1955   June. Secretary of Defense, Charles E. Wilson, issued
a directive which would allow members of the military
the option of having "E. O." (Eastern Orthodox) im-
printed on their identification tags.

1956   Members of AHEPA strove to arouse support for the

self-determination of Cyprus and the release of
Archbishop Markarios from prison. They similarly
urged that telegrams be sent to the United States
Department of State to protest the British policy in
Cyprus. There were, at this time, approximately
72,000 members of AHEPA throughout America.

1957   January. Archbishop Michael delivered the invocation
at the presidential inauguration. He was the first
Greek Orthodox archbishop in America to have done so.

1958   St. Michael's Home for the Aged was founded by the
Ministerial Association of the First Archdiocesan
District and dedicated by Archbishop Michael.

The Pappas Gymnasium was added to the campus of
the Hellenic College in Brookline, Massachusetts.

The Byzantine Fellowship was founded for the purpose
of preserving the Byzantine culture in the Western
Hemisphere. The Fellowship was founded in the Greek
Orthodox Parish of the Archangels in Stamford, Connec-
ticut. The organization sponsors the publication of
Byzantium which appears quarterly.

The Orthodox Church mourned the death of Archbishop
Michael who had been the spiritual leader of the
Archdiocese of North and South America since 1949.

1959   The Holy Synod of the Ecumenical Patriarchate desig-
nated the former Metropolitan James (Iakovos) of
Melita as the archbishop of North and South America.
At the time of his appointment, he was serving as the
representative of the Ecumenical and other Greek
Orthodox Patriarchates in the Headquarters of the
World Council of Churches in Geneva, Switzerland.
He was enthroned as head of the Greek Orthodox
Church in the Americas on April 1.

The House of Trustees of Holy Cross decided to ex-
pand the collegiate department into a four-year liberal
arts college. The first class of the College of Liberal
Arts matriculated in September 1961. The course of
study in preparation for the priesthood had thus been
extended to seven years: four years in the College of
Liberal Arts and three years in the Divinity School.

There were at this time only twenty states whose
legislatures had adopted a resolution granting the
Greek Orthodox Church the status of a major faith.

Following two unsuccessful attempts to be elected
Democratic candidate, John Brademas, the son of a
Greek immigrant from Messinia, was elected to the
86th Congress. A Rhodes scholar and professor of
political science, with distinguished service in the
United States Navy during World War II, he thereby
began a brilliant career in Washington, D.C. In his
first year as a member of the Congress, he was sent
as a member of the delegation to the First Inter-Amer-
ican Conference in Lima, Peru. In 1971 he was
appointed assistant Democratic whip.

1960   March. The first meeting of the Canonical Eastern
            Orthodox Hierarchs in America took place at the Greek
            Archdiocese.

            The American Hellenic Congress was founded. It is
            a federation of all national Greek organizations in
            the United States, and as such represents the Greek-
            American people when it appears before Congress.
            It also sponsors charitable and civic programs. By
            1975 it had 2,500 branches located in cities through-
            out the United States.

            The United States Department of the Census reported
            that 159,167 foreign-born Greeks were living in
            America.

1964   January. Archbishop Iakovos accompanied the Ecu-
            menical Patriarch of Constantinople, Athenagoras I,
            to the Holy Land for an historic meeting between
            the Patriarch and Pope Paul VI.

            The Centennial of Greek Orthodoxy in America was
            celebrated throughout the year. The closing ceremon-
            ies of the commemoration took place in the Holy
            Trinity cathedral in New Orleans from October 14 to
            17, 1965, on the site of the first Greek Orthodox
            church in the Western Hemisphere, established one
            century earlier.

1965   January. Flanked by President Johnson and Vice President Humphrey, Archbishop Iakovos delivered the Inaugural Benediction at the Capitol.

The Center for Neo-Hellenic Studies (CNHS) was founded in Austin, Texas. It is an organization of Greek historians, scholars and writers who wish to preserve and promote Greek tradition, language and culture in America. CNHS sponsors two annual publications, the Bulletin and the Neo-Hellenika. It also presents the Max Manus Award for Greek literature in the United States and Canada, and the Arthur Sockler Prize for Byzantine and Modern Greek studies.

The immigration law was revised, setting an annual ceiling of 120,000 immigrants from the Western Hemisphere, instead of the previous quota restrictions for individual countries. This resulted in increased emigration from Greece. Until 1964, under the old system, the annual Greek quota was 308, whereas under the new provisions, visa applications from Greeks rose to 8,917 by June 30, 1966.

1966   November. Archbishop Iakovos visited South Vietnam and celebrated an Archieratical Divine Liturgy on Thanksgiving Day for Orthodox servicemen. His Emi- · nence, accompanied by Father George J. Bacopulos and Peter S. Kourides, toured United States Army Bases in Korea, Japan, Okinawa, the Philippines and Hawaii.

1967   May. Archbishop Iakovos asked parishes to offer prayers to commemorate the twentieth anniversary of the Truman Doctrine. Truman had addressed a joint session of Congress on March 12, 1947, asking for an appropriation of $400 million in economic and military aid for Greece.

Spiro T. Agnew became governor of Maryland, an appointment he held until 1969.

Bishop Iacovos of Catania was appointed bishop of the Eighth Archdiocesan District. Diocesan offices were relocated from New Orleans, Louisiana, to Houston, Texas.

The American Committee for Democracy and Freedom in Greece was founded in New York City. It is a polit-

ical organization whose main purpose is to unite
Greek-Americans opposed to the military dictatorship
in Greece. It is also concerned with preserving the
Greek language and culture in the United States and
with informing Americans of the situation in Greece.

The American Society for Neo-Hellenic Studies was
established in New York. Its primary function is to
promote knowledge concerning Greek historical and
cultural studies. It sponsors the quarterly publication
of the Newsletter and a monthly lecture on contemporary Greek immigration to the United States.

1968   The first Greek-American was elected to the office of
vice president of the United States. At that time,
serving as governor of Maryland, Spiro T. Agnew
shared the Republican ticket with Richard M. Nixon.

The national origin system for immigrants was abolished. From then on, visas were issued on a
first-come, first-served basis.

A scholarly organization, the Modern Greek Studies
Association (MGSA), was founded in Princeton, New
Jersey. It sponsors meetings and lectures devoted to
modern Greek subjects, and supports scholarly publications. It also serves as a center of information
on courses, programs, activities, and opportunities
in the field of Byzantine and modern Greek studies.
Its primary publication is The Modern Greek Studies
Association Bulletin.

1970   Archbishop Iakovas was presented with the Clergyman
of the Year Award by the Religious Heritage of America
Association for "his leadership in community and ecumenical activities at home and abroad and for contributions to American religious life."

The Reverend Dr. Leonidas C. Contos, president of
Hellenic College, received the Gold Medallion for
"Courageous Leadership in Intercreedal Relations,"
which was presented by the National Conference of
Christians and Jews.

The Bureau of the Census reported that there were
177,275 foreign-born Greeks living in the United

States. This revealed an increase of more than
10,000 over the 1960 census figures.

George Christopher was installed as the first Orthodox co-chairman of the National Conference of
Christians and Jews.

1971   January. Bishop John (Christodoulos Kallos) was
        consecrated Titular Bishop of Thermon and was as-
        signed to the Houston Diocese, thus becoming the
        first American-born bishop in the Greek Orthodox
        Church.

        March. The archbishop opened a series of celebra-
        tions for the 150th Anniversary of Greek Independence.
        They were held at the Fordham University Auditorium
        at Lincoln Center, New York City.

1972   July. His Holiness Athenagoras I, archbishop of
        Constantinople - New Rome and Ecumenical Patriarch,
        died in Istanbul.

        July. The Greek Orthodox Archdiocese of North and
        South America held its 21st Biennial Clergy-Laity
        Congress in Houston. It was to mark a "Double
        Jubilee", celebrating Athenagoras's 50th year as a bis-
        hop and the 50th anniversary of the American archdio-
        cese. At the news of His Holiness Athenagoras's
        death, the congress adjourned in mourning.

        September. The Orthodox Theological Society in the
        United States sponsored the second International
        Conference of Orthodox Theologians at St. Vladimir's
        Seminary in Yonkers, New York.

        The Atlantis ceased publication. It was first published
        in 1894 by Solon Vlastos.

1974   John Brademas, United States congressman from
        Indiana, received the Cross of the Holy Sepulchre
        from His Eminence Archbishop Iakovos, for "his ex-
        traordinary efforts and concern on behalf of the Greek
        Cypriot refugees."

        Greek-American organizations began unifying under
        the leadership of Andrew Athens, first president of

the United Hellenic American Congress. The fighting
in Cyprus was the event which encouraged these
organizations to set aside their differences. Among
this group's main supporters can be included New
York shipowners George Livanos, Pericles Calliman-
opulos and the Goulandris family.

The Hellenic Council of America was founded by
Columbia University Economics Professor Phoebus
Dhrymes. He formed this organization for the express purpose of enlisting academic and professional
people in the campaign to aid Cyprus.

Because of the situation in Cyprus, Greek-Americans
temporarily suppressed their ideological and personal
differences to unite either for the purpose of raising
funds to help the large Cypriot refugee population or
to support lobbying of the United States Congress.
The two best known lobby groups that developed were
the United Hellenic American Congress and the American Hellenic Institute. The latter organization has
a full-time lobbyist in Washington, D.C., and is
headed by Eugene Telemachus Rossides, the son of a
Greek mother and a Greek-Cypriot father.

Archbishop Iakovos founded the Philoptochos Foster
Parent Project to help orphaned and homeless children
in Cyprus. He also urged all Greek-Americans to
write to their congressman to let them know that they
would not sanction Turkish aggression against Cyprus.

1975   The Holy Cross Orthodox Press was founded in Brookline, Massachusetts. Reverend N. Michael Vaporis
is the managing editor. The press publishes a range
of materials from popular to scholarly in the sphere
of Orthodox religious doctrine, history, ethics, worship and scholarship.

The first Greek Orthodox convent in America was
opened at St. Basil's Academy in Garrison, New York.
Called the Greek Archdiocese Convent of St. Iakovos,
it was officially opened when His Eminence, the
archbishop, conducted the Thiranixia Services. The
Convent welcomes women who want to serve in the
Church as nuns.

There were seventeen Greek-American day schools in the United States functioning under the Office of Education of the Greek Orthodox Archdiocese. Of these, ten were located in the greater New York area, one in Washington, D.C., three in Chicago, and one each in Lowell, Tampa, and Houston.

According to the Annual Report of the Immigration and Naturalization Service of 1975, 128,924 Greeks came to the United States between 1966 and 1975.

1976   June. The Cathedral of the Holy Trinity in Manhattan had its interior renovated at a cost of half a million dollars. In accordance with ancient Byzantine custom, Archbishop Iakovos officiated over the traditional rites. The renovations were executed by artist and designer Sirio Tonelli.

October. In one of his election speeches, Carter pledged his support for majority rule in Cyprus and stated that as president he " would do everything in his power to see that the conduct of foreign affairs of this nation would be based on the rule of law and the highest standards of morality." Carter continued: "Just as we believe that there be majority rule of the peoples of Africa, that there also be majority rule for the people of Cyprus." As the governor of Georgia, Carter protested to Washington, D.C., about the Turkish invasion of Cyprus, requested steps to be taken for the protection of Cypriot refugees, and supported a drive to raise funds for these refugees in Georgia.

October. Greek-American journalist Takis Theodora-kopoulos was sentenced to fifteen months imprisonment in absentia for asserting that the Athens English-language newspaper was on the payroll of the KGB, the U.S.S.R. intelligence service.

The Maliotis Cultural Center was added to the campus of the Hellenic College and Holy Cross Greek Orthodox School of Theology. The contemporary glass-walled edifice was built in part with white marble from Greece. It houses a sizable auditorium and numerous exhibition halls for the presentation of cultural and intellectual programs.

1977   February. The Press and Information Office of the
            Greek Consulate in New York held a reception to
            publicize its efforts to promote modern Greek
            studies in the United States. Some of the honored
            guests attending this function were: Prof. Athan
            Anagnostopoulos, in charge of the Modern Greek Pro-
            gram at Boston University; Prof. Lily Macrakis, Pres-
            ident of the Modern Greek Studies Association; Prof.
            Adamantia Pollis, Professor of Political Science at
            the New School; John Nicolopoulos, Director of the
            Greek Press and Information Service; Prof. L. Komitas,
            Professor of Education and prominent anthropologist,
            of Columbia University; Prof. Malefakis; Professor of
            History at Columbia University; and E. Funderburke,
            Senior Development Officer at Columbia University.

            February. "Treasures of Cyprus", a major exhibition
            of archaeological and cultural history, was on tour
            in the United States as a Bicentennial tribute of the
            government of Cyprus. The exhibition opened in
            New York and was then shown in other major American
            cities.

            March. During a ceremony honoring B. J. Marketos
            for his thirty years of service to the Greek-American
            community as publisher of the National Herald, it
            was announced that Eugene T. Rossides would become
            the new publisher of the newspaper. Among those in
            attendence at the celebration were: Menelas Alex-
            andrakis, the Ambassador of Greece; Zenon Rossides,
            Cyprus' U. N. Representative; Charalambos Chris-
            tophorou, the General Consul of Cyprus; Germanos,
            the Metropolitan of Ierapolis; AHEPA's Supreme Pres-
            ident Microutsicos; and the Hellenic Times publisher,
            Harry Stathos. The president of the United States,
            the prime minister of Greece and the president of
            Cyprus each sent a personal message congratulating
            Marketos.

            March. Under the title "Noemata" (Concepts), the
            first broad-based exhibit of works by Greek-American
            artists was shown at the Brooklyn Museum. Fourteen
            contemporary artists of Greek descent exhibited their
            work, seven of whom were born in Greece, six in New
            York City, and one in Turkey. The artists were: Ste-
            phen Antonakas, Tom Boutis, Chryssa, Nassos Daph-

nis, Cristos Gianakos, Steve Gianakos, Mary Grigor-
iades, Aristodemos Kaldis, Aris Koutroulis, Michael
Lekakis, Lucas Samaras, Nicholas Sperakis, Theodoros Stamos and Theo Stavropoulos. The catalogue
viewed the exhibition as an indication that " the
Greek-American community has begun to find the time
and the resources necessary to extend itself into
the arts.

March. On the first anniversary of Greek World Magazine, the first Annual Greek World Awards were presented in New York City. The awards were given to
five distinguished Greek-Americans: Athena Dallas-
Damis, a well-known journalist and translator of
Nikos Kazantzakis, author of The Island of the Winds;
Dino Anagnost, the widely celebrated conductor of
the Metropolitan Greek Chorale; Harry Mark Petrakis,
an author, whose latest volume is an account of the
time of Greece's struggle for independence and which
is entitled The Hour of the Bell; Dr. Ioannis Vassiliou
Yannas of M.I.T., a brilliant scientist who has most
recently worked on the development of artificial skin;
and Nicholas Gage, the well-known New York Times
investigative reporter, author of The Bourlotas Fortune.

September. Maria Callas, famous prima donna of the
opera world, died in Paris at the age of 53. Born in
New York to Greek immigrant parents, she was taken
back to Europe as a child and did not make her United
States debut until 1954. At her death, it was said that
throughout her whole career she sang only leading roles.

A new Greek-American daily newspaper, Proini, began
publication.

George Kotzias, the much-decorated and courageous
scientist, died in New York. He achieved world-wide
fame for his discovery of the most effective drug
against Parkinson's disease. More recently, he was
responsible for establishing a chain of cooperation
between the leading American and Greek institutions
concerned with cancer research.

A chair in memory of the illustrious Greek-born conductor Dimitri Mitropoulos, who died in 1960, was
established at the New England Conservatory of

Music in Boston. His American debut as a conductor was with the Boston Symphony in 1936.

H. Haralambopoulos, the Greek National Tourism Organization director for North and South America stated that the 1977 increase in tourist traffic from the United States to Greece was likely to be as high as twenty to twenty-five per cent. On the basis of present calculations, he considered that the year 1978 would produce a further increase of twenty per cent.

DOCUMENTS

GREEKS IN AMERICA — 1873

The following article was published in the
New York Times. Although the big wave
of Greek immigration began a decade later,
it gives an indication that Greeks were
being recognized as a new ethnic group
in America.

Source: New York Times, August 4, 1873.

THE GREEKS IN AMERICA

GREEK SAILORS — THE PRINCIPAL GREEK COLONIES —
THEIR LOVE FOR THEIR NATIVE LAND

Comparatively little is known about the Greeks in America. Reference is made occasionally in the daily Press to the Greek merchants
of the City, whose enormous transactions in cotton and grain form
an important item in the exports of the country, but beyond that we
seldom see a Greek name coming before the public in the daily in-
cidents of this cosmopolitan city.
Greece is so thinly populated that she can hardly spare any hands to
emigrate to foreign countries, and we seldom see any Greeks among
the nationalities mentioned in the regular reports of our Commissioners
of Immigration. Yet a great many Greeks arrive daily on our shores,
but they come under the quality of sailors, working their passage
on board sailing ships of various nationalities.
As soon as they land here they apply to their Consul in this City,
Mr. D. N. Botassi, for work, when with few variations, the following dialogue takes place:

"When did you arrive?"

"This day."

"Any particular profession?"

"None."

"What do you expect to do?"

"Anything, your Excellency."

"Have you got any money?"

"Not a cent, your Excellency."

"Where are your lodgings?"

"Our traps are at the door; we shall go
  anywhere your Excellency will send us."

"Can you speak English?"

"Nothing but Greek, your Excellency."

There are two sailors' boarding houses in this City doing a thriving
business. The Consul invariably sends them there, and it seldom
occurs that they do not find work in a short time. They begin by doing rough work in loading and unloading merchandise at our piers,
and being generally very temperate, they soon accumulate some
savings.

Their first care is to send the little which they can spare to their
families in Greece. The family ties are so strong among all her classes, particular the lower ones, that even years of absence in foreign
lands cannot diminish their love for their native land and the dear
ones they have left behind. The love of their country is one of the
strong characteristics of the Greeks; they emigrate under compulsion
to better their condition, but the hope to return one day to their
country under more comfortable circumstances is always strong and
paramount.

Few of the Greeks who arrive at this port go West to become agricul-
turists. This means to become in time owners of land whereon to build
their new home. But, as we said before, the Greek has always the
hope to return one day to his country. They mostly go to Chicago,
where they easily find work in loading vessels and navigating the
lakes. On the water they find themselves happy, being in their element. As soon as the lakes are frozen in the Winter time they go
down the Mississippi River, and many of them are working on the
steamboats plying between St. Louis, Cincinnati, Louisville, Cairo,
and New-Orleans. Over 200 of them are to be found in the Crescent
City, where they seem to be thriving under the more genial climate,
not dissimilar to that of their own country. They have all sorts of
professions; many are fruit dealers, keep little restaurants and
coffee houses, where the American bar is combined with little tables
a L'orientales, round which are seated Greeks talking all at the same
time generally, all the idioms of the Greecian Archipelago, drinking
coffee, and smoking paper cigarettes. Many of them are oyster dealers and oyster fishers, owning generally their little craft, which they
navigate themselves, and trade all among the coast from New Orleans
to Indianola and Matamoras, or on the other side through the lakes

to Mobile and Pensacola. The writer tasted, some years ago, an
excellent glass of sherry cobler made by a Greek bar keeper on one
of the steamboats on the Alabama River. In New Orleans the Greek
colony is important enough to maintain a church of their own religion,
built some five years ago by subscription, and divine service is
celebrated every Sunday in the Greek language by a priest educated
in the National University of Athens.
The Greek colony in San Francisco numbers about 300 members, and
is the best organized of all the Greek colonies in the States of the
Union. They maintain a little chapel of their own, and have established a benevolent society. This latter was rendered necessary from
the quantity of newcomers of their countrymen to the Golden State,
with the hope of finding gold in abundance. It is strange with what
great expectations these children of Hellas go to California, and
their disappointment in not finding gold in the streets of San Francisco can be better imagined than described. They seem utterly
astonished when they are told that they must work in San Francisco,
as everywhere else, to gain their living, and the idea of gold is so
deeply rooted in them, that many go to the mines of California and
Oregon with the hope of enriching themselves one day by some sudden smile of fortune. Even in those distant localities they do not
forget their native land. They write to their families in Greece from
time to time, and are subscribers to Greek newspapers, to learn the
news. To the positive knowledge of the writer eight copies of a Greek
newspaper are sent to Greek miners in Piscer County, California, and
a Greek roaster of pea-nuts in Galveston, Texas, is a subscriber to
one of the best Greek newspapers. The only subscribers in America
to an Ecclesiastical Review, published in Athens, are an American
Episcopalian clergyman in New-York and a Greek boarding-house
keeper in Chicago, Ill.
There are no students from Greece in this country, with the exception
of one, who is studying agriculture at the expense of the Greek
Government, in the Illinois Industrial University, in Champaign, Ill.,
on the scanty allowance of $40 per month.
The average salary of sailors, on board Greek vessels, is about $10
per month; it is no wonder, therefore, that those who come to this
country are hesitant to go back, getting as they do, from $30 to
$40 per month. But they get even more on land. Last year a Greek
vessel arrived at this port from Sicily with a cargo of brimstone. The
crew, consisting of twelve men, refused to go to Havanna, where
the vessel was bound, and remained in New-York. They soon found
their way to Athens, below Albany, where they engaged to work at
the railroad depot. They have worked there for one year, saved $300
each, which they sent to Greece through their Consul, and worked
their passage home recently on an American vessel. Their abstinence
from drinking and their hard work were much remarked by the employees
of the railroad.

But the most remarkable incident of the strength of family ties among
the Greeks which came to our knowledge is that of a Greek boy who
came to this country thirty years ago. He was educated for the ministry and pursued his avocation. A year ago he made inquiries about
his relatives in Greece, and finding that a sister of his, a widow,
was still living, but very poor, he opened a correspondence with her.
They have never seen each other, but the expatriated Greek felt an
inherent duty to assist her. He sends her now very regularly a year-
ly pension, with which she lives at present comfortably in Athens.

                          . . . .

There are twelve commercial Greek houses in this city, dealing
largely in cotton, grain, and East India produce; four more are in
New-Orleans, similarly engaged; one in Mobile, one in Memphis,
Tenn., and two in Boston, Mass. These latter deal principally in
Mediterranean produce,mostly dried fruit from Constantinople and
Smyrna, exporting thither New England rum, machinery, and Yankee
notions.

AN INDEPENDENCE DAY CELEBRATION IN NEW YORK

1893

Every year Greeks all over the world
celebrated April 6, as Independence Day
in order to commemorate the historic up-
rising against Turkish oppression.

The New York Times refers to the date of
Independence as April 6, 1827, but it is
in fact the year 1821 that is being celebrated — the day when the Greek flag
was raised against Turkish rule.

Source: New York Times, April 6, 1893, p. 9.

GREECE'S INDEPENDENCE DAY

This is Why The Flag is Floating Over City Hall

A few days ago Mayor Gilroy received a letter from Solon Vlasto,
President of the Greek Society "Athena", asking him to have the
national flag of Greece displayed on the City Hall April 6, the anniversary of Greek Independence. In his letter Mr. Vlasto recalled the
aid that the citizens of New York had given those who were fighting
for liberty in Greece in 1827.

A meeting of citizens was then held in the City Hall, about
$50,000 was subscribed, and three vessels, the ships Chancellor
and the brigs Six Brothers and Jane, were sent to Greece laden with
provisions.

Through Secretary Holly, Mayor Gilroy replied that he would be
very glad to comply with the request, but that as the time was so
short the city would not be able to produce a Greek flag.

Mr. Vlasto at once sent word that he would furnish the flag, and
it will be displayed on the City Hall to-day.

In his letter thanking the Mayor and Mr. Holly, Mr. Vlasto
said:

"I might add that on the Acropolis in Athens, above the noble
ruins of the Parthenon, every Fourth of July the Stars and Stripes
float as a remembrance of the debt of Greece to America."

GREECE'S FREEDOM CELEBRATED

Source: <u>New York Times</u>, April 3, 1893, p. 8.

    The white and blue flag of Greece floated of the City Hall yester-
day for the first time. It was placed there at the request of the Greek
Society in honor of the sixty sixth anniversary of the freedom of
Greece.

    Another flag hung in front of Reiner's Hall, 475 Pearl Street,
where nearly 300 Greeks met to celebrate the day. After a speech
by the President of the society, S.J. Vlasto, the Greeks marched
to Broadway by way of Chambers Street, up Broadway to Canal Street,
and along Canal Street to South Fifth Avenue, where they took an
elevated railway train and went up town to the Greek Church, in
Fifty-third Street between Eigth and Ninth Avenues. Here a service
of thanksgiving was held. . . .

THE GREEK COMMUNITY IN CHICAGO

1909

This account of the Greek community in
Chicago, one of the largest Greek settlements in America, was written by Grace
Abbott, director of the League for the Protection of Immigrants.

Source: "A Study of the Greeks in Chicago,"
American Journal of Sociology, November 10, 1909.

Appreciating that its immediate neighborhood was becoming Hellenic, an investigation of the Greeks in Chicago was made by Hull
House in order that with reliable information about their housing
conditions, their occupations, their family life, and their ambitions,
the resources of the House could be made more useful to its new
neighbors. For this purpose, in a preliminary investigation made last
summer (1908), 350 Greek residences were visited and 1467 Greeks
counted on the schedules. These were not confined to any one neighborhood, but were representative of the city's entire Greek population, the wealthier as well as the poorer. During the winter and
spring a Greek-speaking woman was employed by Hull House to do
systematic visiting among the Greek families of its neighborhood and
among the Greek boys of the downtown district. Upon the information
thus secured by Hull House this study is almost entirely based.

The largest settlement of Chicago Greeks is in the nineteenth
ward, north and west of Hull House. Here is a Greek Orthodox
Church; a school in which children are taught a little English, some
Greek, much of the achievements of Hellas and the obligation that
rests on every Greek to rescue Macedonia from the Turks and Bulgarians; here, too, is the combination of Greek bank, steamship
ticket office, notary public, and employment agency; and the coffee
houses, where the men drink black coffee, play cards, speculate
on the outcome of the next Greek lottery, and in the evening sing
to the accompaniment of the Greek bag-pipes or — evidence of their
Americanization — listen to the phonograph. On Halsted Street,
south of Harrison, almost every store for two blocks has Greek
characters on the windows; and recalling one's long forgotten college Greek, one learns that the first coffee house is the 'Cafe Apol-
lon,' and that their newspaper, The Hellas, is published next door.
A block west, on Blue Island Avenue one finds the 'Parthenon Barber
Shop' and a Greek drug store. If an American were to visit this

neighborhood on the night of Good Friday when the stores are draped
with purple and black, and watch at midnight the solemn procession
of Greek men march down the streets carrying their burning candles
and chanting hymns, he would probably feel as though he were no
longer in America; but after a moment's reflection he would say that
this could be no place but America, for the procession was headed
by eight burly Irish-American policemen and along the walks were
'Americans' of Polish, Italian, Russian, Jewish, Lithuanian, and
Puritan ancestry watching with mingled reverence and curiosity this
celebration of Good Friday; while those who marched were homesick
and mourning because 'this was not like the Tripolis.'

Although the Greeks have scattered much more widely over the
entire country than the Italians and most other immigrants, still
they are little known or understood. They have suffered both here
and in Europe from extravagant praise or unreasonable criticism.
Before the Civil War, in the days when the Native American or Know
Nothing Party flourished, many good Americans were afraid that the
immigrants, who then came principally from Germany and northern
Europe, were going to destroy our institutions and ideals, and there
was organized opposition to their admission. Now the fear is that,
because the immigrants are coming from southern and eastern Europe,
those prophecies of sixty years ago are about to be fulfilled. The
average American, expecting every Greek to have the beauty of an
Apollo and the ability of a Pericles, and reading only sensational
newspaper accounts of some crime he may or may not have committed,
concludes that the race has degenerated and constitutes a most undesirable addition to our population. This is manifestly unfair. The
Greek immigrant should be accepted for what he is worth in modern
society. And we should inquire not only as to his moral standards,
his capacity for self-government and his economic value, but, equal-
ly important, whether his development in these directions is being
promoted or retarded by the treatment he receives in the United
States.

The only way of measuring the morality of a people is by the very
low test of their criminality. For this the only statistics available
are the records of the courts, police departments, and penal institutions. These need most careful interpretation. Classifications
are usually very carelessly made and do not distinguish between
American of native and foreign parentage, so that no conclusions can
be drawn as to the effect which residence in the United States has
upon the conduct of a foreigner. It should also be remembered that
the immigrant's offence is too often only his ignorance of the English
language, which to an irritated Irish policeman is in itself a crime.
Violations of city ordinances through ignorance of sanitary regulations,
of the requirement of a license for peddlers, and of similar regulations,
cause more arrests than viciousness. The newly arrived foreigner

must speak through an interpreter, and a careless translation often gives the court an incorrect idea of what has been said. The testimony of the witnesses against him, and occasionally the charge, are not translated to him, and so he is unable to appreciate the full bearing of the questions asked him, and his chances for acquittal are fewer than the American's. The report of the Commissioner General of Immigration for 1908 shows that 15,323 aliens were detained in various penal and reformatory institutions of the United States. Of this number 196 were Greeks. In the north central group, which includes Illinois and eleven other states, 40 Greeks and 2570 other aliens are reported to be detained. These figures undoubtedly do not give the number of alien criminals for the entire year, but they seem incredibly small even for any one time of the year, when it is remembered that they include alien adult and juvenile offenders held in municipal, county, state, and federal institutions. In Chicago those Greeks who go out to work on the railroads from April to November and spend four or five months in idleness in the city, although not counted in the official census, are probably the ones who are found most frequently in the municipal courts, charged with disorderly conduct. The fact that so many of the Greeks are independent peddlers and merchants instead of employees in some large factory is in part some explanation of their difficulties. Hotheaded and independent, they are, like the Irishman, drawn into disputes which often end in serious quarrels. Undoubtedly their criminal record in America is worse now than it will be in the future. The Greek is one of the last to come to this complex population of ours and the colony as a whole is still ignorant of our language and customs. The young men and boys have been coming in large numbers during the past eight years, and women are following as the men graduate from work on the railroads to the proprietorship of a fruit stand or restaurant. Still a very large proportion of the Greeks are men between the ages of twenty and thirty — the sex and age of the greatest criminality in all nationalities. This very large proportion of men makes the life of the Greek colony entirely different from that of a people who have been coming for the last thirty or forty years. The men who are here alone must live together in large groups, without the restraining influences which come with normal family relationships. Certainly this would account for much of the immorality with which Greek men have been charged. In this respect they are worse than at home, due probably to the demoralizing effect which living in a city's congested district, where invitations to vice are on every side and where there is no counter claim or attraction of a home, always has on men or women. The most hopeful sign is that the Greeks who have been in the country for some time are coming to appreciate this and are trying to make their fellow-countrymen realize the danger which the situation presents.

Considered from other standpoints, the Greek is a most desirable immigrant. With the political training he has had at home, he should be able to adapt himself quickly to our republican institutions. Industrially he is a positive asset in the United States.

Because the colony is so largely masculine, large numbers of the men live together, keeping house on some cooperative arrangement, and from what may be called 'non-family groups' to distinguish them from the ordinary 'family group' in which the wife or daughter does the housekeeping for the family and a lodger or two. Three-fourths, at least, of the laborers and peddlers belong to these non-family groups, while probably nearly the same proportion of the owners of ice cream parlors and restaurant keepers belong to the family groups. This shows very clearly how the system works. Like other foreigners, most of the Greeks must first serve an apprenticeship in the gangs that do the railroad and general construction work for the country. But their apprenticeship is shorter than with most nationalities. A labor agent, who supplies two or three thousand foreigners a season for this sort of work, says that the Greek seldom 'ships out' more than once or twice. In that time he has learned some English and has accumulated enough money to venture on a small commercial enterprise for himself. He becomes a peddler, perhaps later owns a fruit stand and finally an ice cream parlor. By this time he is ready to send for his wife and children, or some Greek woman who becomes his wife, and they are able to live comfortably and happily. During the short time he has been in Chicago the Greek has established his reputation as a shrewd business man. On Halsted Street they are already saying, 'It takes a Greek to beat a Jew.' Historically there is, of course, some reason for this. Mahaffy, an authority on ancient as well as modern Greece, says of the Greeks: "They are probably as clever a people as can be found in the world, and fit for any mental work whatever. This they have proved, not only by getting into their hands all the trade of the eastern Mediterranean, but by holding their own perfectly among English merchants in England.' That they will become great business and professional men in the United States there can be little doubt. They come, willing to do any kind of hard physical work, but thriftily take advantage of every opportunity for advancement.

The testimony of those experienced in teaching immigrants is always favorable to the Greeks. The teacher of the 'adult room' of the Jones School, which is just outside the loop in the downtown district, had 81 Greeks enrolled in 1908-09 out of a total of 252. She said of all the different nationalities represented in the room 'I think I have found the Greeks the brightest and quickest to learn.' At Hull House they have been eager and intelligent members of the regular classes and the men have shown ability in the organization and management of large clubs and classes for themselves.

The patriotism of the Greek is one of his most prominent characteristics and takes very often the exceedingly boastful form usually credited to 'Yankees' in English novels. They are always ready to tell you of the superiority of the Greek soldier over any other, and the men who have been to college in Greece speak of American schools and American scholarship with almost German contempt. A small Greek boy was sure that he won the affection of his Irish schoolteacher by showing her pictures of 'the Athens.' Most of them feel it their duty to spread the fame of their noble race wherever possible. Approving of Hull House, they succeeded in convincing the Bulgarians, for the time at least, that it was intended for the Greeks alone, and the first Greek boy who went through the juvenile court felt that he had added to the glory of the Greek name and dignified that worthy American institution as well. While somewhat exasperating at times, this enthusiastic devotion to their mother country is after all a most desirable characteristic and one which the Anglo-American should readily appreciate.

Considering their Eastern training and traditions of almost Oriental seclusion, the Greek women adapt themselves very quickly to American customs. A Greek Women's Club has been meeting at Hull House once a week as a Greek Women's Philanthropic Society has been formed there by the more prosperous, who expect to help in various ways the unfortunate members of their colony. This charitable organization is eagerly encouraged by the men, for the Greeks, although extremely shrewd in their business dealings, are at the same time generous. They give liberally to one another in times of sickness or unemployment. On Tag Day for the children's charities of the city the women reaped a good profit in the Greek stores and coffee houses on Halsted Street. When three small Greek children were left without homes, it was not difficult to find Greek families in the neighborhood of Hull House who were willing to receive and care for them temporarily or indefinitely.

Unlike the Italian women, they do not work outside their own homes or at sweatshop work. Out of 246 Greek women and girls over fifteen who were visited in the investigation, only 5 were found to be at work. This is not alone because the Greek men usually succeeds in business, but because he considers it a disgrace for his wife or his sister to work, and the entire family often suffers that this tradition that 'the women must not work' may be upheld. An example of this came to the attention of the League for the Protection of Immigrants this spring. A Greek man about twenty-five years old sent his brother-in-law, who was ill with tuberculosis, back to Athens. His sister and her two children, both old enough to attend school, were left in Chicago. The sister was able to work, but this her brother would not consider. Although he had a very small income, he rented a flat for her, paid her bills, and finally with some help from

his friends purchased tickets for her and the children to go back home.
The women was not a very good mother or sister, and the man had
little affection for her, but he knew that he would have been disgraced
in the eyes of the Greek colony if the 'sacred tradition,' as Professor
Andreades of the University of Athens calls it, had not been upheld.
The women are good housekeepers. The Greek houses are almost
uniformly clean and comfortable, and the women and children neatly
dressed. Even in non-family groups the houses are often well kept
and the food well prepared by the men themselves.

The non-familiy groups living above barns and feed stores were
the only ones found in dangerously unsanitary conditions. The men
who live in this way are usually peddlers who keep their horses in
the barns. Over one such barn there were fifteen peddlers. They were
all unmarried, between 20 and 30 years old. They earned an average
$10 a week and paid $30 a month rent for the barn and the rooms
above it. The rooms were unfurnished and dirty. The men slept on
mattresses on the floor. This was often the condition in which groups
of peddlers were found, but there were some exceptions. In one
group twenty-two men lived together. They had rented five of the six
apartments in the flat building. Ten of these men were laborers who
worked for the Rock Island and received from $10 to $12 per week,
and eleven were peddlers who estimated their weekly profits at $9.
Each one of the men paid $4 a week, which went toward the payment
of rent, food, and the wages of the man who was cook and general
caretaker of the group. With one exception all of these men were
under thirty, and they were all unmarried. The flats were kept clean
and the men lived comfortably. Often the owner of a restaurant, a
fruit store, or a shoe shine parlor furnished his employees board and
room. For example, the owner of a restaurant had a nine-room flat
where eight waiters, who worked for him and were paid from $6 to
$10 a week, lived with him. The house was comfortably furnished
and clean. All the men were unmarried and between twenty and thirty
years of age. In another group were five laborers who paid $12 a
month for a four-room rear house. These young men came from Tripolis. One of them had been here three years and was able to read
and write English. The other four were attending night school. The
house was clean and gave the general impression of thrift and industry.

In the non-family groups the Greek boy presents a special
problem. The boys often come with some neighboor who passes as
their uncle or father and are apprenticed to one of their fellow-
countrymen. They work as bootblacks, help around fruit stands, or
peddle fruit and vegetables. That many of these boys are worked
under a system of peonage there can be little doubt. Some evidence
of the existence of this and a few cases where boys have suffered
gross physical abuse from the older men with whom they lived have

come to the attention of the League during the past year. And in
addition to these very ugly possibilities an investigation of the
shoe shine parlors in the Loop District of Chicago showed the danger
of their general mode of life. The ages of these bootblacks range
from 13 to 36, the majority being 17. Their hours of work are extremely long. In addition to their board and clothes, the usual wages
paid those boys is from $15 to $20 a month. An employer who has
a large establishment or several small ones, as many of them do,
has to provide housing facilities for a number of boys. One man,
for example, has eleven rooms — two floors and the basement —
for twenty-five boys. The rooms are clean and neatly furnished and
the food abundant. Another has eleven rooms for twenty boys, with
an old Greek man in charge as cook. This place is not clean. There
is no furniture except beds, and a long table in an inside room which
serves as a dining room. Here the boys were found one night between
half-past nine and ten o'clock. They had just returned from work and
were eating their supper of soup and stewed corn. The danger of
this life can be readily understood. The boys spend nearly all their
waking hours at work. They live, as many of the poor must, near
immoral neighborhoods and are easily accessable to men and women
who wish to accomplish their ruin. They have no time for regular
attendance at evening classes or clubs, no normal life or relationship. But for the discipline of the bosses, who want them to be ready
for work the next day, an even larger number would find excitement
and relaxation in dangerous amusements. Hard as the lot of these
boys is, it is better than that of an apprentice in Greece. This accounts for the fact that the parents of the boys as well as the boys
themselves are satisfied with the terms on which they work, and
consider deportation a great hardship. They work for long hours
cheerfully, confident that in a short time they will be in a position,
not to work fewer hours, but to set up as independent business men
for themselves.

"The Greeks, then, upon acquaintance prove to be bright, in-
dustrious, and capable men and women. Better than some, and not
so well as others, they are meeting the dangerous temptations which
come with long hours and unwholesome living conditions. What they
become as a result of their American environment should be an American responsibility. The best way to help them and the city is not
by the general condemnation which is too often meted out to 'the
stranger within our gates,' but by recognizing their ability, industry,
and capacity for good citizenship and uniting with them to suppress
the vice and exploitations from which they suffer.

MOB ACTION AGAINST GREEKS IN OMAHA,
NEBRASKA - 1912

Idle railroad workers in South Omaha had
created some problems in that area, and
the murder of a policeman resulted in
mob action against the Greeks. The following article describes in detail the only mob
action ever recorded against Greeks in
America.

Source: Roberts, Peter. New Immigration, 1912,
Macmillan, p. 299.

In South Omaha, one of the most shameful riots ever known took
place because of prejudice against the foreigner. A Greek went into
the house of a young lady of questionable character, and a policeman, following the man, arrested him without any overt cause what-
soever. The Greek resisted and, in the scuffle which followed, the
officer was shot. That was Saturday night. The following Sunday
morning as the bells were ringing, calling men to worship, a mob
assembled and, under the leadership of disreputable fellows, began
storming the Greek quarters, smashing windows, breaking doors,
and pursuing the terror-stricken and defenseless Greeks in all directions. On the corner of L Street and 24th Avenue was the firm of
Demos Brothers — superior men in every sense of the word, one of
them being married to an American girl. This store was several blocks
away from the Greek quarter, but on came the raging mob as the
surging tide, lashed by gusts of rage and passion. They attacked
the store at a time when the white-haired mother of the Demos
Brothers sat quietly at the soda fountain. They smashed windows,
tore to pieces the soda fountains, strewed on floor and street the
contents of windows and cases and left the place, which represented
an investment of more than $7000, a mass of ruins. The brothers
and their families fled for life. They had other stores in Omaha, which
they immediately gave up, for they knew not how far this wave of
fury, fanaticism, and savagery would sweep, and in a week they
found themselves reduced by mob violence in Christian America from
the position of prosperous merchants to paupers. . . . Instances
of mob violence against the foreigners are also found in the East,
and even the South is not exempt. . . ."

A SOCIAL CASE RECORD
1915

The following case record is an example
of the difficulties encountered by Greek
immigrants.

Source: Abbott, Edith. Immigration: Select Docu-
            ments and Case Records. New York: Arno
            Press, 1969, pp. 623-624.
Peter Ganos, Seven Other Greek Men, and
            an Employment Agency

June 16, 1915. — Complaint made by eight Greek men [names and
addresses omitted] living near Hull House against the Immigrant Employment Agency, 800 Canal Street. The men told the following
story to A.V. [Greek visitor]: They paid $40 ($5.00 each) to the
employment agent two weeks ago and were promised jobs on the
following day. The next day they went to the office, and the agent
said, "No work." The next day they went again, and the next day
they went, and they were always told there was no work. They asked
then for their money back. They have gone to the agent many times,
and he will give them no money and no work. Now, Peter Ganos himself and three of the other men have got jobs through a friend and
are leaving for Davenport, Iowa, tomorrow. Men left receipts in
office and asked that Mr. X., manager of a Greek coffee house on
Halsted Street, be notified if claim were settled. Later. — Tele-
phoned Mr. Day [State Supervisor of Private Employment Agencies],
and he will investigate.

[The remaining portion of this case record is omitted. Court action
was finally necessary in this case, which was not heard in court
until several of the men had left town. Each of the claims was, however, finally paid and the refund sent on to the men.]

GREEKS IN NEW YORK FORM A VENIZELOS PARTY

1916

At the outbreak of the First World War,
King Constantine of Greece proclaimed
neutrality for Greece while Eleutherios
Venizelos made an agreement with the allies
and formed his own revolutionary government. The political divisions of Greece
were carried over also to the Greek communities in the United States. In fact, the
factional strifes were often carried to such
extremes to nearly result in civil war among
Greeks in America.

The following is an account of the founding
of the Venizelos party in New York City, from
where it spread through Greek communities
throughout the United States.

Source: <u>New York Times</u>, October 16, 1916, p. 1.

GREEKS HERE FORM A VENIZELOS PARTY

10,000 In Hall and Overflow Meeting Organize Nationwide Committee
of 1,000

QUICKLY SUBSCRIBE 4,000

Resolutions Denounce Constantine and Country's "Betrayal" —
Committee of 1,000

With tumultuous enthusiasm and prolonged cheers, followed by the
singing of the national anthem, the Venizelos Party in America was
formed yesterday afternoon at a meeting of more than 3,000 Greeks
in the Hall of the Pan-Hellenic Union at 56 West Thirtieth Street.
Greeks from all over the city and nearby cities attended the meeting.
It was estimated that more than 10,000 flocked to the Union, and
those who could not get into the hall held overflow meetings on the
sidewalk.

All were insistent that the old Government of Greece had tried to
betray their country, and that Venizelos, with his Provisional Government, was destined to be its saviour. When the call for funds for
the assistance of Venizelos was sent out in the hall more than $4,000

was subscribed in less than ten minutes. So great was the enthusiasm
and so earnest was the patriotism that a little bootblack, who went
to the meeting straight from his stand, gave $150.

In addition to the immediate contributions a great number added
their names to the list as willing to give a stated amount, each week
or each month. Last night the managers of the meeting said that the
fund would reach $100,000 within a month, and that similar amounts
would be raised monthly.

Resolutions condemning the old Government and supporting the
Venizelos party were adopted at the end of the meeting, which was
presided over by Petros Tatanis, founder of the National Herald,
a Greek daily newspaper. In his introductory remarks he announced
that the Greeks had been called together to express their sympathy,
support, and allegiance to the Venizelos Government, and to denounce the old Government. He said that Venizelos represented the
"true Hellenism" and the national aspirations and ideals of Greece.
The Venizelos Government represented the real people of Greece. The
shortcomings of the old Government, and the attempt to "betray"
Greece were fully set forth by Mr. Tatanis, and much applause followed his presentation, which consisted of high praise of Venizelos
and his patriotism.

Audience Shows Patriotism

Dr. R. Dadakis of 258 West Forty-third Street appealed to the
patriotism of the audience, and was greeted with cheers and the
promise of support of the movement. C. Vassardakis, former Consul
General, the last speaker, took up in detail the scope and purposes
of the organization.

It was explained that this was the first meeting of a nation-wide
movement in which more than 100,000 Greeks, in every city of the
United States had agreed to join. Practically 90 per cent of the
Greeks here, it was said, were heart and soul in favor of the Venizelos Government, the others being "followers of the King." All
the speakers disapproved of King Constantine and roundly denounced
him.

Following the speaking the collection was taken up. Several
hundred of those who were unable to give as much as they wished
put their name down as volunteers for Venizelos's army. As one of
them said later, "If we cannot give money to help Greece, we will
give our lives for her salvation."

The resolutions were adopted without a dissenting vote and with
great enthusiasm. Summarized these were as follows:

"Whereas the Government of King Constantine has abandoned
more than $30,000,000 worth of forts and munitions in Macedonia
and allowed the Fourth Regiment to be kidnapped, and has thus dis-

honored Greece and all Hellenism: in addition it has cast a stain
on the national honor or Greece and its policy threatens the extinc-
tion to the nation.

"The Greeks of New York and America resolve, in mass meeting,
to endorse and support the Government in accordance with the Constitution headed by Venizelos, against the present Government. They
pledge allegiance to the Venizelos Government, which the Greeks in
America consider the only salutary movement, and for the supports
of which they will do everything in their power.

"They greet with enthusiasm the heroic islands, Crete, Eamos,
Mitylene and Chios, for having embraced this movement. They send
their greetings to the National Defense Committee in Soloniki, for
its efforts toward the liberation of our country.

Nation-Wide Movement

"They exhort the Greek colonists in America that through meetings,
resolutions, and other measures they use their great moral influence
to induce the other parts of Greece to also embrace the national
movement and to expel the enemies who abolished the Greek sovereignty in Macedonia, and also to defeat and cast out the demagogues now
surrounding the King."

A Committee of One Thousand was formed to carry on the work of
the organization, numbering among its members many of the most
prominent Greeks in this City.

Among those who attended the meeting and who signified their
intention of taking the lead in the movement were Dr. D. Callimachos,
editor of the Greek Herald [sic], who was decorated by King Constantine for his services with the Greek Army; N. Gallanson, agent of the
Greek Steamship Line; Petros Tatanis, a merchant; George Georgopou-
los, a tobacco merchant; S. Sofioanopoulos, a merchant from Athens
now residing here; Dr. A. Alexian, D. C. Carousos, President of
the Pan-Hellenic Union; Chrys T. Kontos, a member of the firm of
Caracands Brothers; Thomas Ravazula of Ravazula Brothers, and
M.B. Atheneos, a tobacco merchant of 59 Pearl Street.

GREECE URGES CITIZENS TO ENLIST IN U.S. ARMY
1917

> Greece had never recognized the American
> citizenship of her emigrants in contrast to
> most other European countries. She insisted
> that her former citizens serve in her army
> and considered them Greeks who were only
> absent temporarily. The following account
> showed a new attitude of the Greek govern-
> ment.

Source: New York Times, December 27, 1917.

GREECE URGES CITIZENS TO ENLIST IN OUR ARMY

Promises to Recognize Such Service as Rendered to Their Own
Country.

Washington, Dec. 26.— Greece wishes her citizens in the United
States to enlist in the American army. Not only will she suspend
punishments which ordinarily would follow the enlistment of Greeks
with a foreign power, but she will reward them for supporting the
American cause. This is the substance of a note from the Greek
Government delivered today to the State Department.

The following communication has been addressed by the Greek Legation here to Greeks in the United States:

"The Royal Legation of Greece brings to the knowledge of Greeks
residing in the United States that, according to a decision of the
Greek Government, a collective and previous authorization has been
granted to all the Greeks wishing to enlist in the American army.

"No legal consequences, therefore, would be applied in such cases,
the Greek Government considering any Greek enlisted in the American Army as serving in the Greek Army.

"Furthermore, any Greek serving in the American army who shall be
mentioned for gallantry, being considered as fighting in the Greek
army, will be rewarded by the Greek Government.

"This collective authorization is extended to all the Greeks who
have already enlisted in the American army without previously
applying for the authorization required by the Greek laws."

THE COFFEE HOUSE – A BRIEF DESCRIPTION
1930

The Greek immigrant brought with him many
traditions which left their mark on the devel-
oping American culture. Perhaps the most
significant of his earlier gifts to this country
was the coffee house. As noted in the chronology section of this book, the Cretan Konopios opened the first Greek coffee house in
New England in 1652. Since then, these establishments have opened in one town after
another, across the United States. The life
associated with the coffee house and Greek
business acumen are briefly touched upon in
the following article which focuses on a dance
popular among coffee house patrons.

Source: Outlook, May 14, 1930, pp. 48, 49, & 75.

▶▶ Kyotchek ◀◀

By STOYAN CHRISTOWE

AMERICA is nursery for many out-
landish customs and institutions.
The floods of peoples that poured
in upon these shores and spread over
the vast expanse of continent carried
foreign tastes and predilections which
have left their impress on American life.
To be sure, as fast as they came America
stripped the immigrants of their gay cos-
tumes and alien appendages, such as
beards and moustaches, but their deeply
imbedded traits and characteristics could
not be rubbed out with the same ease
and readiness. As a consequence, customs and traditions, many by now
abandoned and forgotten in the old
countries, have been engrafted in this
country and have thriven with amazing
persistence. It is not unlikely that at
some future date foreign ethnologists

studying the past customs and habits of
their people may have to come to America to observe living examples of the
same.

Of the many heterogeneous institutions which the more recent immigrants
to America transplanted upon the chaste
soil of this land probably the most exotic
and the least known about is the "kyotchek"—a terpsichorean revelry brought
here from the classic shores of Greece
and the quaint, weird coffee houses of the
Levant. In its place of origin, kyotchek
has gone the way of the yashmak, the
fez, and other semi-Oriental appurte-
nances which draped with mystery and
speckled with color and glamor the Near
Eastern world. There the word kyotchek now remains merely the name of a
dance entertainment that one saw twenty

years ago. But in America, despite the abundance and diversity of amusement, kyotchek found a nourishing soil and a healthful climate. For a generation it has enjoyed a popularity in Balkan and Near Eastern colonies throughout the United States, particularly in the Middle West, where immigrants from these parts of the world are settled in larger numbers.

Kyotchek is superimposed upon the coffee house. What the playhouse is to the play the coffee house is to kyotchek. Happily, then—or otherwise some would insist—coffee houses were established in this country simultaneously with the influx of immigrants from those countries in which they existed. Their introduction is not to be wondered at. Nearly all immigrants from southeastern Europe and from Asia Minor came here without their families; they came as people go to a gold rush, or to a boom place; they came to fill their pockets with gold and return to their homelands. But many stayed, and for every one that went back two fresh ones arrived.

Unlike the immigrants from the northern parts of Europe, these swarthy people from the southeast, who invaded America in large numbers, were farther removed from American culture and civilization. Their advent was regarded as an intrusion and resented by the northerners who had preceded them. In many is alive the memory of days when they could not walk out of their quarters without being "tomatoed" or otherwise assaulted by unbridled youngsters, or "dagoed" and "God-damned" by their fathers. Settled in the more obscure sections of the cities where they created tiny worlds of their own, they soon felt the need of places where they could gather to talk and while away the tedious hours of immigrant existence. The opening of coffee houses patterned after those in the old countries was but natural. Here at least they could shut themselves in and find respite from the American world.

B UT THAT THESE Oriental *tembelanés* should have enjoyed a steady growth over a long period of time and developed into a considerable business in a country seized with the spirit of

material creativeness and harassed with maniacal activity is a phenomenon. The coffee house is indigenous to the sluggish Oriental who keeps no track of his time. In it one sits for hours dozing over his cup of Turkish coffee and lazily drawing at his narghile. Yet in this country, wherever there are twenty Armenians, or Greeks, or Bulgarians, or Assyrians, there one is bound to find the anachronistic coffee house. And there, amidst the clatter of the riveting machine and the furious tempo of a material civilization the narghile is kept gurgling and the dice rattle in the *tablah*.

In cities like Chicago, Detroit, St. Louis, where there are large colonies of Balkan immigrants there are coffee houses for the different strata of immigrant society—dingy places for the menial workers and luxuriously appointed parlors that cater to the intelligentsia and the business class.

A coffee house is generally located in a big hall either on the first or second floor of a building. It is furnished with marble-topped tables and chairs with wire-twisted legs. The walls are decorated with the pictures of old country statesmen with whose policies the patrons are in agreement. In a community of Venizelists pictures of the late kings of Greece are not in view. In Macedonian coffee houses one sees portraits of comitadji chieftains. At the back end of the hall there is a small kitchen where the proprietor brews the coffee and the tea which he himself serves to his patrons. "Lokum," "baklava" and other Oriental delicacies are also served, in addition to bottled American soft drinks.

In those coffee houses equipped for kyotchek presentations there is a small stage near the kitchen. And it is here the interesting performances take place. Whoever has seen (and who has not in the movies) an Oriental potentate seated on a soft divan and gazing rapturously at his favorite odalisk wriggling and twisting her sinuous body has a fair idea of what kyotchek is.

The commercially-spirited Greek immigrants may boast credit for the importation of this bacchanal to the chaste shores of America. Slightly altered from the original version, having yielded to such influences as American jazz has exerted upon it, the kyotchek has been elevated by the astute Greeks from a dubious pastime to a highly profitable business with a semblance of respectability about it. It may well rank as one of the minor amusement enterprises in America, though the Americans themselves know nothing of it.

The kyotchek troupe consists of two girls and three men, the latter making the orchestra of a violin, a clarinet and a xylophone. The girls, mostly American born, schooled by the managers to sing obscene Turkish and Greek songs and to dance the sensuous kyotchek, are generally plump of body—a discernment on the part of the producers, they having taken into consideration the tastes of their patrons, whose esthetic appreciations have not escaped the influence of long cohabitation with their Oriental masters.

Unable to speak the languages of the Near East, the girls learn the songs by heart and sing them with zeal and animation. After each number the girl having sung or gone through the contortions of the kyotchek passes the tambourine from table to table for the patrons to drop nickels and dimes in it. No admission having been charged, the attendant of the kyotchek considers it almost obligatory to make his regular contribution.

. . . The troupes now form in Chicago and first present themselves to the critical eyes of the Chicago Greeks. If the girls can "do their stuff" and meet with the approval of the blasé Chicago first-nighters, they are instantly booked for long periods in Halstead Street, the Broadway of kyotchek in America, with contracts for extended and profitable visits to Detroit, St. Louis and other mid-western cities, ready for them to sign. And once a kyotchek girl makes a hit with the Greeks, she need have no worry about her future. Owners of restaurants and ice cream parlors and bootleggers and real estate operators are only too eager to place at her disposal their expensive limousines. She has only to choose.

LOYALISTS v. LIBERALS - 1935

Each political upheaval in Greece sent ripples
of discord to America. The Greek-American
communities were broken into factions, which
fought vehemently. The royalists wanted the
United States to help restore the monarchy,
while the liberals thought the monarchy was
obsolete, and were convinced that an American type of democracy would flourish in
Greece. The article appearing below describes
only one incident, but it illustrates a problem
which affected all aspects of Greek-American
community life.

Source: New York Times, September 9, 1935,
p. 40.

ROYALISTS DISRUPT
GREEK RALLY HERE

Couple and Daughter, 8, Are Hurt
by Blows at Reception of 6,000
Pro-Republicans

EJECTED BY THE POLICE
Other Monarchists Expelled Also
From the Audience of Ex-Premier
After Uproar.

A reception for former Prime Minister Alexander Papanastasiou of
Greece by 6,000 Greek-American republican sympathizers at Mecca
Temple yesterday afternoon was interrupted for five minutes while a
police detail forcibly ejected A. A. Athenson, Greek-American royalist leader, his wife and their 8-year-old daughter for starting a
monarchist demonstration.

Four other royalists were ejected before order was restored, but
no arrests were made. The meeting was thrown into an uproar by the
disturbance, which occurred immediately after Mr. Papanastasiou
had finished speaking.

The Athensons were seated in the third row, to the right of the
speaker's dais. Mr. Papanastasiou had turned to take his seat when
Mrs. Athenson sprang to her feet and asked to be heard. The uproar
followed.

As Demetrius Christophorides, associate editor of the Greek
National Herald and chairman of the reception, attempted futilely
to calm the aroused audience a half dozen stalwart ushers pushed
their way through the crowd to Mrs. Athenson.

Police Rush to Aid.

Her husband sought to protect her and it seemed for a moment
that both were going to be roughly handled, but Police Captain John
Challan of the Fourteenth Precinct fought his way to the centre of
the group. With the assistance of another policeman he managed
to herd the Athensons to the front door of the auditorium, where
they were released.

Meanwhile several other royalists started to demonstrate. Four
of them were pushed up the aisle by ushers and were turned over
to the police, who took them outside and released them. A police
emergency squad assisted Captain Challan and his detail of two
sergeants and ten patrolmen in clearing the street.

Mrs. Athenson was treated at home later by her family physician
for severe shock and bruises, the result of blows she received before the police could protect her. The physician was in the audience
at the time and witnessed the disturbance. Mr. Athenson also was
struck several times in the face and stomach. Anghula, their young
daughter, received a severe bruise on the head.

Cries by Monarchists.

Once the demonstrators had been ejected Mr. Christophrides
quickly restored order. A scattering of royalists in the audience
had once or twice before shouted, "Hurrah for the monarchy!" and
"Hurrah for King George!" Their exclamations, however, had been
received with goodnatured raillery by the republican sympathizers
up to the time the Athensons were ejected.

An ovation was given Mr. Papanastasiou by the rest of the audience. Frequently he was interrupted by cheers. His speech,
delivered in Greek, lasted more than an hour.

Mr. Papanastasiou, according to the translators of his speech,
urged Greek-Americans to support a republican form of government
in Greece and protested attempts being made to restore the monarchy,
which would result, he said, in "the establishment of fascism in
Greece" and would "greatly impede her national progress."

"Democracy has not failed in Greece," he declared. "There is
no activity looking to the improvement of the people that has not
been improved on during the last ten years under a republican form
of government."

Tells of Gains by Republic.

Mr. Papanastasiou asserted that "production under the democracy has been doubled, savings have been increased, constructive social legislation has been enacted, educational methods and equipment have been greatly improved, many refugees have been cared for and practically all classes of people have benefited in some way."

A resolution was adopted asking Mr. Papanastasiou to transmit to the Greek Government a declaration that a majority of Greek-Americans favor a continuation of the present form of government in Greece. It also asked for the reinstatement of all State employees and university professors discharged as an aftermath of the attempted revolution of last March; that a general amnesty be given all Greek political prisoners and exiles; that the present National Assembly be dissolved and a free election held and that the Greek Government end its repressive acts against democratic newspapers, organizations, and leaders.

Mr. Papanastasiou was a guest at a dinner last night at the Hotel St. Moritz. It was given in his honor by 250 Greek-American businessmen, journalists, engineers and other professional men. Another reception will be held for him tonight at Columbia University by Greek students there.

GREEK TRADITION IN AMERICA - 1937

The Greek immigrants brought with them
to America a deep rooted religious and
cultural heritage. The following article
which appeared in the Travel Section of
the Sunday New York Times describes
one of the traditional rites of the Greek
people. This particular celebration takes
place in Tarpon Springs, Florida, a fishing village whose population is composed
to a great extent of Greek-Americans.

Source: New York Times, January 3, 1937,
Section XI, p. 4.

SPONGE MEN ON HOLIDAY

Tarpon Springs Divers Enact Old Greek
Rite of Baptized
Crucifix

By Dora Byron

Cassadaga, Fla.
On every Jan. 6 in Tarpon Springs an ancient Greek custom is revived in Cross Day. It is observed now only in the Greek Islands
and in this sponge fishing village of Florida. For a day the price
of sponges, the diver whose life-line fouled, and the "hooking"
boats that will never return, are forgotten. Choirs chant. Incense
floats lightly in the air. Reflections of crimson robes and gold
banners ripple on the bayou.
It is Epiphany at Tarpon Springs. The Florida sun is warm on
the up-turned faces of hundreds of Greek visitors as they await
the ceremony of the "baptized crucifix." At that time a cross will
be dropped into the deep blue water of the bayou. Dozens of
bronzed divers will plunge as one, in a race to recover it. He who
brings up the cross receives the Greek Orthodox Archbishop's
blessing.
Early in the morning of Jan. 6 worshippers congregate at the
Greek church of St. Nicholas, where masses are said until noon.
Then, with the Archbishop of the church at its head, a procession
is formed. Majestically it wends its way to the waters of Spring

Bayou. Giant candles flicker. Gilded insignia of the church glow
in the sunlight. Rhythmically the choir sings its Epiphany praises.

Procession to the Docks

In the procession walk the archbishop, wearing his jeweled
mitre; Greek priests, in the bright rich robes of their office; visiting
Episcopalian rectors, adding a touch of white, and alter boys,
carrying banners. Behind them the victors follow. Solemnly they
pass through tropical streets to the dock, where the day before
picturesque Greek boats unloaded their sponges.

On a small craft near the bayou docks sit rows of silent, muscu-
lar young men, the divers. Much of their lives has been spent with
the fleet of 150 fishing boats, perhaps hooking the sponges from the
surface, perhaps diving. They watch the procession draw near.
Who will be the swimmer to receive the blessing? The priests arrive. They take their places on the divers' barges. With dark eyes
fixed on the archbishop, the divers stand poised.

The crowd listens as passages are read from the Bible, in Greek
and in English. At the conclusion, a white dove is released over
the water. Eyes squint as the bird circles and swoops. But the
dove is soon forgotten, for, after a brief ceremony, a cross flashes
into the deep bayou. Like a streak of brown the divers are after it,
sliding swiftly out of sight.

Recovery of the Crucifix

Tensely, the visitors wait, heads uncovered. The water is
broken as, one by one, the men reappear on the surface. And one
diver is eagerly waving a bronze arm. The sun glints again on the
crucifix. The choir breaks into a chant as the lucky diver kneels
on the barge before the archbishop. "The blessings of the waters"
are believed assured by the ceremonies of Cross Day.

A special ceremony is also observed in Tarpon Springs at Easter
time, which, figured according to the old Greek calendar, does not
fall on the same date as the Roman and Protestant Easter.

Except on these occasions groups of the little thirty-five foot
sponge boats are always out on the Gulf of Mexico, perhaps fifty
or eighty miles from land. Their trips may last for several weeks
or months, depending on the "crop."

Sponge receipts some years for the skeletons of those jelly-like
animals are nearly $850,000. In addition to this it is estimated that
from $50,000 to $75,000 worth are sold annually outside the exchange. Thus, Tarpon Springs is one of the largest sponge markets
in the world.

GREEK IMMIGRANTS IN THE UNITED STATES
1941

This account, written almost sixty years after
an earlier one, describes a known entity.
By now, the Greek population in the United
States had become sizeable and contributed
largely to the cultural aspects of this country.

Source: Louis Adamic, Commonweal Magazine,
        vol. 33, January 31, 1941, pp. 366-368.

Greek Immigration in U.S.

What they do, what they contribute,
what they think.

The drastic events of the past half-dozen years, now achieving their
climax in an inclusive world crisis, have underlined in our national
consciousness an important American fact - namely, that this country
is humanly an extension not only of the British Isles, Ireland, Holland, France, Germany and Africa, as it was at its inception, but
of all Europe, and, in a lesser way, also of parts of Asia.
    The developments originating in Germany, with their culminating
world-wide repercussions, have made us aware of our vast German
and Jewish elements; the Munich crisis, of the considerable Czech
and Slovak groups; the early weeks of the Second World War, of the
four or five million Poles and Polish Americans; the Russo-Finnish
war, of the 400,000 Finnish immigrants and their American-born
children; and the conquest of Denmark, Norway and Holland, of our
Danish, Norwegian and Dutch groups. Mussolini's dramatics and
adventures have, of course, made us keenly conscious of our Italians and Italian Americans even further back than a half dozen years
ago; and now his invasion of Greece, or rather his fiasco in that
connection, makes us strongly and pleasantly cognizant of the
Greeks and Greek Americans in our midst.
    And, in consequence of these events, the various new-immigrant
elements and tens of millions of individuals belonging to them have
become intensely aware of themselves as German, Jewish, Italian,
Czech, Slovak, Polish, Finnish, Danish, Norwegian, Dutch and
Greek Americans — in most cases without the objectionable hyphen;
the name of the old-country nationality is used merely as an adjective
describing their backgrounds. This is, I believe, a significant thing
in our national life, as yet inadequately appreciated by the country
as a whole, but claiming almost my entire attention since late in 1938,

when I embarked on a five-year survey and study of the subject. It
is at once a sound and a dangerous development: sound because as
a country we tend, thereby, to move away from the old but still ener-
getic idea that the diversity of our population is something to be be-
moaned and toward the newer idea that the diversity may be indeed
a great advantage; and dangerous because, if we don't exert intelligence in connection with it, the dynamics of the idea are such that
they are apt to lead to new or enhanced cleavages among our people,
to an intensification of nationalisms and separatisms of our new-
immigrant groups, which will not result in anything desirable. . . .

So much by the way of a hasty, too hasty, preface to this brief,
too brief, article I am asked to write on the Greek element in the
United States for this special issue of The Commonweal. My "Greek"
files contain pertinent material for at least ten times the space which
the Editors allow me here, and I may as well say before I begin that,
my limitations being what they are, I can offer but a few highlights
of the Greek story in this country which, in good part by virtue of
the Albanian events, is of a sudden clearly destined to assume growing importance in the minds of approximately 1,000,000 of our fellow
inhabitants who are of Greek origin and descent, and therefore, if
for no other reason, should interest all of us.

The Greeks are among the newest of the New Immigrants. One of
my most valued informants, Mr. Peter T. Kourides, of New York,
attorney for the Greek Archdiocese in North and South America, be-
lieves that prior to 1890 there probably were fewer than 100 persons
of Greek origin and descent in the United States. Among these early-
comers were the distinguished Calvocoressi family, one of whom became Commandant of Midshipmen at the United States Naval Academy in Annapolis. The current head of the family, the roots of whose
tree reach into the Byzantine period, is Mr. Leonides J. Calvocoressi,
a member of the New York Stock Exchange (many Greek Americans
seem overproud of this fact), whose son married a few years ago a
direct descendant of one of the signers of the Declaration of Independence. Another distinguished pre-mass-immigration Greek was
Michael Agnos, whom Samuel Gridley Howe brought to this country
as a little boy and who later founded and directed the Perkins Institute for the Blind in Boston.

Some of the New England Perkinses, generally regarded as Anglo-
Saxon, are said to be descendants of a Greek merchant named Per-
kentzis who came to the New World, via London, in the 1780's, and
whose family later changed the name to Perkins. In Trenton, New
Jersey, there is a Perdikaris Street, named after a member of the
Perdikaris family, which was founded by another early Greek settler
in the United States.

Not a few early Greeks went South and, in the first half of the
eighteenth century, became important in the development of the

American tobacco industry, notably the cigarette. This was due to
their tobacco background in the Old World.

Most of these pre-1890 Greek immigrants were brought here by
American Philhellenes who went to Greece during 1821-'30 to fight
for her independence, a la Lord Byron, in the wars against Turkey.
It may be noted, too, that during this period such Americans as
Daniel Webster and James Monroe made speeches asking for funds
for the Greek patriots battling for the freedom of their country. In
Boston, the old South Church became the headquarters for Greek re-
lief.

Since 1890, nearly a half-million Greeks came over. At first they
tended to segregate in and about New York City and in New England,
where large Greek colonies were formed in Boston and Lowell, Massachusetts, and in Manchester, New Hampshire. Subsequently, considerable Greek settlements appeared in Philadelphia, Chicago and
Detroit. Now there is hardly a community of any size in the United
States without Greeks or Greek Americans. Early in the 1900's, as
I tell at some length in my book "From Many Lands," the Greek
sponge fishermen "invaded" Tarpon Springs, Florida, and turned
the little resort town into the sponge capital of the Western Hemisphere.

The overwhelming majority of the post-1890 Greek immigrants
were humble folk, like the majority of immigrants of all other nationalities at the turn of the century and later. They were unskilled workers
needed in the textile mills and shoe-manufacturing plants of New
England and in various industries in such centers as New York,
Philadelphia and Chicago. I have stories of violent warfare between
Greek immigrants and the Irish, who, assuming priority rights for
themselves, resented their intrusion. For a decade or two in many
New England communities nothing was lower than Greeks in the esti-
mation of non-Greeks, especially the Irish. The old-time immigrants
who now tell of those days smile; one of them recently said to me,
"We fought with the Irish only in self-defense when their attitude
and tactics became completely unbearable." The old wounds still
smart, but since the early 1920's the tendency has been for those
animosities to vanish. Lately the events in Albania operate here
and there in the United States to turn Greek immigrants and their
American-born children into pets.

The Greek immigrant seldom made a career of hard manual labor.
As soon as possible, and this particularly in the larger cities, he
went into some sort of business, opening a restaurant, a flower
shop, or a confectionery or fruit store. Often, like the Jewish newcomer, he started in business as a street vendor, selling if nothing
else, shoelaces. Now there is a rare town of any size that hasn't
a few Greek restaurants, candy-stores or flower-shops. Most of
these establishments, especially restuarants, are of no very high

quality: not a few, however, attained to excellence. In the larger cities the Greek restaurants, flower-shop and confectionery-store owners are oganized in powerful associations.

Greek immigrants have made important contributions to the confectionery and soda-fountain business. They have invented and developed the use of fruit syrups. One of them is said to have brought over nothing less than the ice-cream cone, which he had invented in London. And some Greek American historians of my acquaintance are emphatic in crediting the invention of the ice-cream sundae to Greek genius.

Immigrants from Greece and their American-born descendants have gained a strong foothold also in the theatrical business. The name of Alexander Pantages comes most readily to mind in this connection. Two years ago Stellios Cocalis died, leaving a fortune of more than $2,000,000 as a result of his operation of some fifty theatres in New York and New Jersey. In Chicago, Harry Rekas, Van Nomikos and John Manta control strings of successful movie houses, while in upstate New York J. Dipson is important. But the topmost Greek theatrical tycoons are the Skouras brothers who together control approximately 600 theatres, 200 of them in Greater New York. Spyros Skouras is usually near the top of the list of the largest income tax-payers in the United States. In 1939 his income as President of the Fox West Coast Theatres alone was near $500,000. In the same year, his brothers Charles and George paid taxes on more than $300,000 each.

Facts of this sort are not specially exciting to me; I retail them here because they are impor tant not only to the Horatio Alger heroes I have listed and the few others in their economic class, but— extremely so — to the Greeks and Greek Americans generally. Such facts are important to all the new-immigrant groups and to most of the individuals belonging to them as they grope about in the American atmosphere and inside themselves for evidence that they belong here, that they have within them the ability to advance themselves in the American way —alas! the most obvious American way.

So let me give a few more such facts about the Greeks. A few have succeeded greatly in the hotel business, particularly in New York; and in the shoe-retailing and fur trades. A Greek American is looking over my shoulder as I write, and he reminds me that I forgot to mention by name the famous and numerous Foltis food shops in New York, which are establishments started by two enterprising Greek immigrants. I am asked, too, to mention the Karzis brothers, who operate two million-dollar ballrooms in Chicago. And I mustn't forget Nick the Greek, a gambler known from coast to coast, now in Hollywood, who has won and lost tens of thousands of dollars in single nights, and has popularized Plato, his favorite author, among the highbrows of the underworld.

Now enough of Success!

All of the 500,000 Greek immigrants, of course, did not stay
here. After making a little money, many returned to Greece. The
preponderance of those who stayed in this country remain humble
folk. They skate on the thin ice around the edges of our erratic e-
conomy. Along with most of the other new-immigrant elements, they
are "marginal" people, whether they are in business or not. Their
families are large, and the numerical estimates of the second generation run as high as 750,000.

Most of the immigrants and many of their American-born children
are strong adherents to the Greek Orthodox Church, whose Bishop
in the Americas is a power among them. The immigrants have a score
or more of Greek-language newspapers. Recently, a young New
Englander named Constantine Poulos began to publish, in Washington (where he is a Government clerk), an English-language monthly,
the Hellenic Spectator, in which the younger generation tries —
not uninterestingly — to examine its Hellenic background.

In Washington, too, is the headquarters of Ahepa, the Greek
Americans' largest fraternal union, which has also a cultural function
among them. It stands for Hellenism, the traditions and values of
Greece, which it holds are essentially identical with the ideals of
Americanism.

Many Greek Americans have Anglicized or simplified their names.
Many were more or less ashamed or uneasy about being Greeks. The
Albanian war has changed that to a large extent. They are shedding
their old inferiority feelings. This war is doing for the Greek Ameri-
cans what a year ago the Russo-Finnish war did for the Finnish
Americans.

I know a great many Greek Americans personally all over the
country. Most of them are excellent, delightful people. But my
favorite person among them is an elderly immigrant I know in a small
city in upstate New York. He came to America to escape persecution
and terror in Asia Minor. He owns and runs a pitifully small confectionery and variety store. He complained to me that he worked
hard and long hours, and that he was getting old and tired. I asked
him why he did not have his 14-year-old son help him more in the
store. He turned on me, almost angrily: "What do you think I am!
My boy will stay in school. He must study at home after school. He
must be a good student; he must become a good man. There is much
wrong here; we must make a better America. My son must go to
college, the best there is. Me — I don't count. My life is over.
How shall I say it? I realized myself by coming to the United States.
Now I must help my children, so they will help this country — so
they will know what to do — help make it great."

AN ACT OF CONGRESS - "E.O."
TAGS - 1955

The struggle to allow members of the United
States armed forces the option of choosing
Eastern Orthodoxy as their religious preference and to have "E.O." indicated on their
identification tags was long and intricate.
It culminated with the passage of the Congressional bill reproduced below.

Source: Congressional Record, May 2, 1955.

84TH CONGRESS
1ST SESSION
H. R. 5940

IN THE HOUSE OF REPRESENTATIVES

MAY 2, 1955

Mr. DORN of New York introduced the following bill; which was referred
to the Committee on Armed Services

A BILL

To allow certain members of the Armed Forces to designate
the Eastern Orthodox faith as a religious preference on
their identification tags.

1   *Be it enacted by the Senate and House of Representa-*

2   *tives of the United States of America in Congress assembled,*

3   That the Secretaries of the Army, the Navy, and the Air

4   Force are directed to authorize the inclusion of the Eastern

5   Orthodox religious faith as one of the religious faiths au-

6   ˙thorized to be designated as a religious preference on iden-

7   tification tags issued to members of the Armed Forces. The

8   capital letters "E. O." shall be used on such tags to indicate

9   the designation of such faith.

ADDRESS BY SECRETARY HERTER BEFORE AHEPA
Washington, 1960

Source: U.S. Department of State Bulletin,
vol. 42, pp. 516-517. April 4, 1960.

AMERICA'S DEBT TO GREECE

It is most gratifying to see around me the faces of so many of my friends and former colleagues in the Congress. On an occasion like this it is a little hard to believe that I have been away from the Hill at all.

It is indeed a pleasure to attend the national banquet of AHEPA, membership in whose Boston chapter I am proud to claim. Because I think of myself as one of you, I take this occasion to announce that I plan to make a visit to Athens within a few weeks. I expect to stop there on the fifth of May, following the NATO meeting in Istanbul.

Greece is a land of many beauties, created both by nature and by men. The genius of the Greek people is expressed not only in the monuments of their culture but also in their friendliness and charm. Not least in these endowments are their gracious and devoted King and Queen. I look forward to a pleasant and relaxing opportunity to renew my acquaintance with a beautiful country and with many good friends.

I am here tonight to acknowledge a debt. Not to pay it, because that is beyond my power, but to acknowledge it and thereby give an indication of its nature and magnitude. The debt is the debt America owes to Greece. It is a debt of many aspects, intellectual, artistic, political, human. It is a debt not alone for knowledge and ideas but above all for inspiration, for examples of excellence, beauty, and courage.

The United States has been very much aware of its debt to Greece from its beginnings as a republic, for the Greek tradition is the wellspring of our own freedom. Thus we have sought where we could to offer repayment. Since I happen to be a graduate of Harvard, I think particularly of the efforts of Edward Everett, a Harvard man who like myself was an editor, a Congressman, a Governor of Massachusetts, and United States

Secretary of State. Edward Everett was for a time professor of Greek literature at Harvard, hence he enjoyed a full awareness of the glories of that legacy. It was he who led the widespread movement for American popular support of Greece during her War of Independence. From 1821 to 1830 there were contributed from all over this country clothing, medicine, and financial support to relieve the suffering of the rebirth of freedom in the ancient nation where freedom was born.

It would be an error, however, to think of Greek sacrifices in the cause of freedom only in terms of events a century or more past. The fierce and courageous dedication to freedom displayed by the Greek people during the Second World War and after it was both inspiring in itself and important to the broader effort. Here again we sought to help in what ways we could, in gratitude for the contribution in blood and gallantry being made by the Greek people to our own security and freedom.

Moreover in the time since then Greece has played and continues to play an essential role in the strength of NATO as the shield of Europe. Just as the size of a nation in area, population, or resources does not necessarily determine the magnitude of its contribution to ideas and culture, so the size of a member of an alliance does not in itself give a measure of its value to the alliance. Interdependence creates an equality among partners which our Nation gladly and, may I say, humbly acknowledges.

The contribution to the life and achievements of this country by Americans of Greek descent is, like the contributions to freedom of Greece herself, not only a matter of the past but of the present and future. Two symbols of this are the presence with us tonight of a young member of Congress of Greek descent and the recent announcement of plans to found a Hellenic University of America.

And the ideas of the ancient Greeks, like the descendants of the ancient Greeks, have their contribution to make to events today. The Greek orator Isocrates, addressing the Olympiad of 380 B.C., said, "The name of the Greeks is a symbol not of who we are but of what we are. He who shares our culture is a Greek." Since the very essence of the culture to which Isocrates referred was political and intellectual freedom, his words apply today. He who shares the love of freedom, with all that freedom entails culturally and politically, is today not alone a Greek, nor an American, but a citizen in full standing of the community of the free. That is the animating spirit of NATO and of other associations for the defense of freedom. That must be the governing spirit of this country's relations with any nation which has freedom or hopes to gain it.

It is clear that this same spirit is reflected in the ideals and service of AHEPA. It seeks at once to promote the better understanding of true Hellenism and to encourage loyalty to the United States. It was founded by and for Americans of Greek descent, but its ranks include leaders in American life from many backgrounds. The causes served by AHEPA over the years have ranged from relief to victims of flood and hurricane in Florida, Mississippi, and Kansas City to war and disaster relief and health and educational support in Greece and other areas of the Middle East.

The annual AHEPA excursion, which sails for Greece tomorrow night, is a useful means of strengthening the bonds that exist between the citizens of the community of the free. President Eisenhower said last year that today the country needs more individual diplomats from Main Street traveling abroad as part-time ambassadors to help build understanding as a foundation for lasting peace.[2] I particularly congratulate AHEPA for the 25,000 volumes of American books collected by its chapters, which the excursion will take with it to give to the people of Greece. Even this impressive contribution is, of course, only a token repayment of the debt of culture the world owes to Greece. But it is an important token not only of gratitude but of bonds that remain strong.

So I offer all good wishes to the members of AHEPA at their 14th national banquet; I congratulate you on the usefulness and success of your program; and I urge you to continue, in the future as in the past, your contributions to Hellenism, to Americanism, and to the cause of freedom.

---

[2] For text of the President's remarks before the Third National Conference on Exchange of Persons, see BULLETIN of Feb. 23, 1959, p. 260.

FIFTEEN YEARS OF GREEK-AMERICAN PARTNERSHIP
1962

Under Secretary McGhee addressed the
16th Biennial Ecclesiastical Congress of
the Greek Archdiocese of North and South
America in Boston, Massachusetts, on
June 26, 1962.

Source: Department of State Bulletin, vol.
pp. 99-100, July 16, 1962.

Fifteen Years of Greek-American Partnership

I am greatly honored by the opportunity to
address such a distinguished group of leaders of
the Greek Orthodox Church assembled here from
both North and South America. It is particularly
fitting for us to commemorate this evening the 15th
anniversary of the Truman Doctrine, which
linked inextricably the destiny of our country with
that of Greece.

It is also a pleasure to speak before the citizens
of the great State of Massachusetts here in the city
of Boston, which is proudly known throughout the
United States as the "Athens of America."

The ties between Greece and Boston are indeed
many. In 1958 one of the world's largest ships,
which was launched at Fore River shipyard in
Quincy, Massachusetts, was named *Princess
Sophie*. Her Majesty Queen Frederika and her
daughter, the Princess for whom the vessel was
named, took part in the christening ceremonies.

I am told that there are more than 85,000 Massachusetts citizens of Greek origin. The Greek
diocese of Boston has more than 50 churches, and
they are well attended and supported.

Greek Independence Day on March 25 is regularly observed in Boston. In 1961, on the 140th
anniversary, some 3,000 persons jammed the auditorium of the Greek Theological School, in the
town of Brookline, where President Kennedy was
born. They came to recall the story of the hard
fight for freedom, to express thanks for the great
achievements and the great promise of modern
Greece, and to join Archbishop Iakovos of North

and South America in a solemn oath to defend liberty, whenever and wherever endangered.

Even those Bostonians who are not of Greek ancestry feel the right to cheer for Greek independence. The revolution that led to Greek freedom in 1821 was, as you may know, substantially supported by Boston citizens. Colonel Jonathan Miller and Doctor Samuel Gridley Howe, both of Boston, went to Greece to join the revolutionary forces. Professor Edward Everett of Harvard University and America's great statesman, Daniel Webster, carried the cause of Greece to the American people.

But the links between our country and Greece are not limited to the State of Massachusetts. They are nationwide. There are many parallels between America and Greece. The Greek people are a democratic and virtually a classless society, as are the people in our nation. Freedom of thought, freedom of religion, freedom of speech—these cherished principles are of the very essence both of the Greek and American spirit. Greece has been enriched by the blended cultural heritages of many lands—as America has been—and this has kept both countries strong and creative and perpetually young.

The record of the Greeks as champions of liberty is longer than ours. But since the birth of the United States, our sons have fought side by side in both world wars and in Korea. We share the special alliance of NATO—the shield of the free world. Despite her internal problems of recovery and readjustment from her wounds during the last war, Greece plays an important role in NATO.

AHEPA CONGRESSIONAL BANQUET - 1964

The following speeches are extracted
from the addresses delievered at the
16th National AHEPA Banquet held in
Washington, D.C. Included here is
the introductory statement of AHEPA
Supreme President, John G. Plumides,
and extensive remarks made by Representative John Brademas.

Source: United States Congressional Record-
Extension of Remarks, April 8, 1964.

HON. JOHN BRADEMAS
of Indiana
In the House of Representatives
Wednesday, April 8, 1964

Mr. BRADEMAS. Mr. Speaker, every 2 years the Order of Ahepa, the
American Hellenic Educational Progressive Association, the leading
organization in this country of Americans of Greek descent, sponsors
a banquet honoring the Congress of the United States.

This year the Ahepa banquet honoring Members of the House of
Representatives and Senate of the 88th Congress was held in Washington, D.C., on March 16.

Among the speakers addressing the 16th National Ahepa Banquet
were Ahepa Supreme President John G. Plumides; Mrs. Josie Chase,
grand vice president , Daughters of Penelope; Pierre Calogeras,
Charge d'Affaires, Royal Embassy of Greece; His Eminence Archbishop Iakovos, Greek Orthodox Church of North and South America;
Congressman John Brademas, of Indiana; Senator Kenneth Keating,
of New York; and Mr. Henry R. Luce, editor and publisher of Life
magazine.

Mr. Luce received on this occasion the Order of Ahepa 1964
Socratic Award for his contributions and services, through a series
of articles in Life magazine, to the dissemination of Hellenic culture and Hellenic ideals to the peoples of the world.

Mr. Speaker, my colleague Congressman John Lindsay, of New
York, has earlier inserted in the Congressional Record - A1522,
March 24, 1964 - Senator Keating's address on this occasion. Under unanimous consent, I insert in the Record several of the other
addresses delivered at the 16th National Ahepa Banquet.

The 16th National Banquet of the Order of Ahepa Hon-
oring the 88th Congress of the United States, Monday,
March 16, 1964, Washington, D.C.
(By Ahepa Supreme President John G. Plumides)

It is a unique opportunity and an unusual one in which the supreme president of our organization assumes the role of toastmaster.
It is no easy task to preside at a podium where so many illustrious
Americans must listen to your humble servant. The Order of Ahepa,
as you know, is an organization composed primarily of Americans
of Hellenic descent. The Ahepa has a history of 42 years of service
to the United States of America, the greatest democracy ever con-
ceived in the mortal mind of man. And it is our fervent hope that
as long as the organization exists, so long as there is blood in the
veins of any American of Hellenic extraction, that the Order of
Ahepa will continue to render service to this great democracy of
ours.

This banquet, which the Order of Ahepa sponsors every 2 years,
is given in honor of the greatest legislative body in the world - the
Congress of the United States of America. These Members of Congress who serve as our legislators, who enact and promulgate the
laws of our land, sometimes are the forgotten soldiers of American
history. But we, in the Order of Ahepa, can never forget the debt
of gratitude that we owe to you, the Members of Congress, for serving the American Nation in a most American form of government.

We are cognizant, my good friends of the Congress, of the times
and conditions that we must face as a nation; and we have full con-
vidence, trust, and faith in your actions to safeguard this democracy
for this and future generations of Americans.

Funeral of King Paul

Only 4 days ago, I had the distinct privilege of attending the
funeral of the late King Paul of Greece in Athens as a designated
member of the official American delegation, selected by the President of the United States, that great American, Lyndon B. Johnson.
King Paul of Greece was a dedicated friend of the United States, a
man who labored long under democratic principles, and who knew
no other ally than the United States of America. He knew no pro-
tector other than the United States of America.

The Order of Ahepa feels deeply gratified that the President of
the United States selected our organization's supreme president to
be a member of the official American delegation to King Paul's funeral. Only in America could an opportunity of this kind present
itself to one who is the son of immigrants from Greece, as I am.
Those of us born of parents who chose America as their new home

have tried, as loyal Americans, to prove our worth as citizens of
this great country that we lovingly call the United States of America.

On that solemn occasion in Athens, where religious and political
leaders gathered for the funeral of King Paul, all nations of the
world were represented, and among those taking part in the funeral
procession was your humble servant. This could only happen in
America.

This is America, and I am grateful to this, the greatest democracy, and to you, the Members of Congress, who represent our people
in this hour of peril throughout the world.

* *

Remarks of Congressman John Brademas, of Indiana

I an honored to have been invited to speak this evening to my
brother Ahepans at this biennial banquet honoring Members of
Congress.

At the outset of my remarks I want to extend my warmest con-
gratulations to Henry R. Luce, on being the first recipient of the
Order of Ahepa Socratic Award for the magnificent series of articles
on ancient Greece published in Life, the magazine of which he is
editor and publisher.

I want also to take this opportunity to salute our dedicated and
hardworking Supreme President of the Order of Ahepa, Brother John
G. Plumides, and to congratulate him on the splendid leadership
he is giving to our organization.

As you know, four of us at this table, His Eminence, Archbishop
Iakovos; Mike Manatos, Special Assistant to President Johnson;
Supreme President Plumides; and I have just returned from Greece
where we, as members of the official U.S. delegation appointed by
President Johnson, attended the funeral of King Paul of the Hellenes.

Though our journey to Greece was a sad one, it was nonetheless
an experience memorable in several ways.

Funeral of King Paul

First, standing in the cathedral, we saw many of the chiefs of state
and kings and queens and princes of Western Europe who had come
to honor the late King.

And we joined with the members of other delegations in marching
in the 2-hour long procession from the cathedral down Hermes Street
through the heart of the city of Athens.

It was, however, an especially proud moment for all of us, as
Americans, to be able to go to Greece on the first official mission
of the gracious and lovely wife of our President, Mrs. Lyndon B.

Johnson.

And I know I speak for the rest of my colleagues in the American delegation as well when I say that we shall long remember having gone to Greece on the first trip to that country of the man who, more than any other American, has come to be a symbol of the friendship of the people of Greece and the people of the United States, President Harry S. Truman.

I am pleased to report to you that both these outstanding figures in our national life were warmly received by the hundreds of thousands of Greek people who lined the streets of Athens to do honor to their late King and to pay homage to their new monarch, King Constantine.

President Truman and Mrs. Johnson

In view of some of the press reports you may have read, you may be surprised to learn that both President Truman and Mrs. Johnson and indeed every member of our delegation were greeted with such friendship in Athens.

I make this observation because I realize, as do you, that the present crisis over the Cyprus issue has caused some demonstrations in Athens that were critical of the United States.

I can only say to you, however, from my own personal observations last week, that I am convinced such demonstrations in no way reflect the overwhelming sentiments of the people of Greece, who continue to look with respect and affection to our own country, as we do to theirs.

Cyprus

I have alluded to the question of Cyprus. Both because I have just returned from Greece and am the only Member of Congress of Greek descent, I think it appropriate that I address myself to the Cyprus issue for a few moments.

It is a matter about which all of us in this room are deeply concerned. I know we must all feel greatly encouraged that the latest news from that island indicates that, in keeping with the unanimous resolution of the United Nations Security Council a few days ago, the first troops of the U.N. Peace Force have arrived and that more are on the way.

I say we must all be encouraged for clearly it would be catastrophic if the political disputes respecting an island of some 600,000 people were to be the cause of all-out war between Greece and Turkey.

1. Such a war would have the most appalling effects in terms of lost lives of the nations directly concerned, Greece and Turkey

and Cyprus.

2. It would mean the destruction of the southern flank of NATO, for both Greece and Turkey, we must not forget, are our allies in the North Atlantic Treaty Organization.

3. Such a war would, in addition, be a major triumph of Soviet foreign policy and a victory achieved at almost no cost to the Communists.

Danger of War

4. A Greek-Turkish war, moreover, would always mean the possibility of involving the two great powers, the United States and the Soviet Union, in direct military conflict, thereby posing the unthinkable danger of a third world war.

5. Finally, the territorial independence and the national sov-ereignty of Cyprus, which all of us here tonight strongly support, would, if full-scale hostilities were to erupt in the eastern end of the Mediterranean, become almost meaningless words.

For all of these reasons, then, we must view the Cyprus issue with more than passing concern and, if I may say so, we must view it not only as men and women of Greek descent, justifiably proud of our Hellenic heritage, but we must view it as Americans, proud of our own Nation and citizenship and soberly aware of the immense responsibilities which history has thrust upon the United States in a troubled world.

I may here interject that the role of a great and powerful nation like ours in a dispute in which two allies are involved is never a happy one for it will inevitably bring criticism from both sides that the keeper of the peace is favoring the other. Without here presum-ing to judge the validity of such criticism, I think we all know that the United States has in fact been criticized by both Greeks and Turks on precisely these grounds.

Truman Doctrine

In 1947, the United States, through the Truman doctrine, an-nounced to the world and to the Soviet bloc in particular our resolute determination to support the people of Greece in their valient stuggle against communism.

Standing last week in Athens in front of the splendid statue of President Truman, given to Greece by our Order of Ahepa and marked by both the American and Greek flags waving at half-mast, I read once more, engraved there, those words of President Truman of exactly 17 years ago this month:

"I believe that it must be the policy of the United States to sup-port free peoples who are resisting attempted subjugation by armed minorities or by outside pressures.

"I believe that we must assist free peoples to work out their own destinies in their own way.

"I believe that our help should be primarily through economic and financial aid, which is essential to economic stability and orderly political processes.

"Should we fail to aid Greece and Turkey in this fateful hour, the effect will be far reaching to the West as well as to the East.

"We must take immediate and resolute action."

Just as the United States made a commitment to the support of freedom against Communist challenge then, so must we reiterate that commitment today in the crisis over Cyprus, for make no mistake, the Soviets have already begun to fish in the troubled waters surrounding that island.

Russian offers of economic aid in recent days, the negotiation of a Soviet air agreement with Cyprus, and the recent visits of Cypriot officials to Moscow are hard evidence of this continuing danger.

President Kennedy's Salute to Archbishop Makarios

None of us questions for a moment the deep commitment of Archbishop Makarios and the Government of Cyprus to maintain the freedom and independence of Cyprus.

I remember well, for I was there, President Kennedy's salute to President Makarios at the White House on June 5, 1962:

"We want to express our very warm welcome to our distinguished visitor who comes from a most ancient country, representing a most ancient people, and also a young country. We salute him particularly because of the long and difficult fight he conducted for his country's independence, involving the most sensitive interests, involving his own persistent, courageous and far-seeing view of his country's future. * * * Your country occupies a most significant, strategic position in the world today. Your own efforts to maintain the independence and viability of your country are well known here, and you come to the United States with the warmest wishes of all of our people who admire a courageous fighter for freedom."

I draw your attention to President Kennedy's reference to President Makarios' "efforts to maintain the independence and viability" of Cyprus for the pattern of Communist takeover in the postwar world must surely provide an object lesson to all nations intent upon maintaining their freedom. Just as we Americans are deeply concerned about what happened in the Caribbean, we must be alert to such dangers in the Mediterranean.

Peaceful Solution

These, then, are some of the major considerations we must have in mind as we reflect on this issue.

Surely we can all agree that we must encourage with every means a peaceful, nonviolent resolution of this dispute.

For we Americans are committed to the conviction that peaceful change is the way to bring change. The success of the Reverend Martin Luther King, for example, in pressing for nonviolent means to solve our own major domestic problem must by now have made that fact abundantly clear. The Senate of the United States is today acting on this matter and, at last reports at least, is doing so in a nonviolent manner.

I spoke of change for I believe there must ultimately be some change in the London-Zurich Agreements of 1960 which are part of the Constitution of Cyprus.

We know now that much of this treaty has proved to be unworkable and indeed has helped cause some of the present conflict between Greek and Turkish Cypriots.

While we can all agree, that, as in our own country, there must always be protection of minority rights, we must also surely agree, again as in our own country, that in a democracy the majority, again respecting the situation of the minority, must ultimately be able to work its will or democracy will become meaningless.

Peaceful Change

Just as our own United States Constitution recognizes the necessity for change -peaceful change- so too I believe we must recognize that change in the Constitution of Cyprus has become essential if that constitution is to be workable.

Because of our commitment to peaceful settlement of international disputes, we must continue our support of the United Nations Peace Force on Cyprus and of the work of a mediator there.

As you know, the United States has already made a commitment of $2 million to the U.N. Peace Force.

For although we might prefer to stand aloof from this dispute, the stakes are far too high in terms of our own national interest and security and in terms of the peril this crisis presents to the free world for us to do so.

Cypriot Cooperation

Let us hope that all the parties concerned will cooperate fully with the U.N. Peace Force and the mediator and will, difficult though it may be at times, act with sober restraint and profound awareness of the potential dangers of failure to cooperate. I was delighted to read in today's paper the airport statement by the Interior Minister of Cyprus, Polycarpos Georgadjis, on the arrival in

Nicosia of the Canadian members of the Peace Force: "The contribution of the U.N. Force to efforts of the Cyprus Government to restore
law and order will be immense."

Greece has a new, young and able monarch in King Constantine
and I am confident that we in the United States are anxious to help
him in his responsibility and to help Prime Minister Papandreou and
the Government of Greece in their efforts to continue the economic
and social progress of the country.

Certainly as prospects increase for the peaceful resolution of
the Cyprus issue, Greece can again turn its attention, with renewed
energy and commitment , to the internal development of the country.

Just as 17 years ago the people of the United States joined hands
with the people of Greece in the defense of freedom against communism, so too the American people stand ready today to work closely
with Greece in meeting the challenges of the present hour.

United States - Greek Ties

As a Member of Congress and as an American of Greek origin,
I am deeply gratified to see Greece develop as a modern, democratic
nation fully capable of handling its own affairs.

The special ties which have linked the peoples of Greece and
America for over a century and a half are still there and are perhaps
of even greater significance today.

If the democracy which our two lands have come to symbolize
is to endure and if the cause of human freedom to which both our
peoples are committed is to prevail, it is in the interest of both the
United States and of Greece that we maintain a constant vigilance
over this special relationship within the alliance.

May I say, in closing, that no organization in American life has
a greater responsibility for the maintenance of this relationship than
has ours - the Order of Ahepa.

I am confident that both as Ahepans and as Americans we will
meet that responsibility.

STATEMENT BEFORE THE SUBCOMMITTEE
ON IMMIGRATION AND NATURALIZATION
1965

The following is a statement which was to
be presented on behalf of the Greek Archdiocese of North and South America before
the Subcommittee on Immigration and Naturalization of the Committee on the Juduci-
ary of the United States Senate on March
24, 1965.

Source: File on Immigration, The Greek
Archdiocese of North and South America.

Mr. Chairman:
     My name is Peter T. Kourides and I am the General Counsel of
the Greek Archdiocese of North and South America. I am submitting
the statement herein at the direction and in behalf of His Eminence
Archbishop Iakovos, the Primate of the Greek Orthodox Church in
the Americas.
     The said Greek Archdiocese has under its administrative and
spiritual jurisdiction 400 parishes in 325 cities and towns in the
United States with 1,250,000 communicants, nearly all of whom
either migrated from Greece or are the first or second generation
descendants of Greek immigrants. The bulk of our people came to
this country within the last 50 years. In this short space of time
they have made important contributions in the arts, the sciences,
the professions, in commerce and industry, in our political life and
indeed in almost every field of endeavor.
     The Greek Archdiocese in the United States sincerely believes
that our current immigration law which is predicated on the discriminatory allocation of quotas by national origin is a cruel anachronism
and a discredit to our nation. This degrading concept of judging a
man on the basis of his place of birth or the racial ancestry of his
parents is unworthy of our country's ideals and aspirations. Discrimination against persons because of their national origin is just as
morally wrong and ruthlessly inhuman as discrimination because of
race or religion. The time has come when the government of the
United States can no longer afford to sanction prejudice by statute.
     It is our further conviction that the vast majority of the American
people long ago rejected the narrow, fear ridden view that is reflect-

ed in the continuance of an immigration policy based on the bigoted national origins concept. Most of our citizens agree with President Johnson that a newcomer to our shores should not be asked where he was born or how he spells his name but rather what he can do for America.

Under the current immigration statutes only 308 Greek quota immigrants may enter this country annually while 156,000 quota numbers are allocated each year to Britain, Ireland and Germany. Many thousands of these non-transferable quota numbers remain unused while Greek non-preference visa applicants wait an entire lifetime without ever obtaining the coveted visa that they are seeking for the opportunity and the privilege to make this country their new home. In 1963 there were a total of 58,876 unused quota numbers while 105,690 Greek immigrants were left waiting on the over-subscribed quota list at the American Embassy in Athens. The obvious implication under the current national origins immigration system is that regardless of individual qualifications a man or woman born in Greece is not as good as someone born in Ireland or England or Germany. This discriminatory system is a source of global embarrassment to the United States. Greece and other nations whose citizens are statutorily discriminated against reject and resent the implication that they belong to lesser breeds.

The New York Times in its lead editorial on January 4, 1965 commenting on President Johnson's reference to immigration reform in his state of the union message to Congress stated:

"Since 1924 the United States has rigged admission to this country on a racist basis. The Nordic countries of northwestern Europe have large immigration quotas while the Slavic and Latin countries of Eastern and Southern Europe have tiny quotas....

Thus it is that the United States stands self-condemned before the world for imposing severe restraints on immigration by men and women from Athens and Rome - two of the chief sources of glory and greatness in that Western civilization Americans share and defend today. The people who produced Plato, Aristotle and Demosthenes are limited to 308 quota numbers a year. The people of Dante and Michelangelo are limited to 5,666. In this fashion the United States solemnly counts and calibrates the potential worth of all mankind. Is there not something terribly arrogant - and also absurd - in this self righteous national posture?"

The Greek Archdiocese in the United States is not seeking any increase in the number of immigrants that are to be admitted annually to this country. We are merely asking for the elimination of the discriminatory national origins quota system which limits admission of only 308 Greeks each year. We support wholeheartedly President Johnson's forthright message to Congress on January 13, 1965 in which he outlined the requisite basic revisions to the Immigration and Nationality Act of 1952. In closing we fervently hope and pray that the 89th Congress will act favorably and expeditiously to adopt the necessary legislation that will eliminate from our immigration statutes every vestige of unfairness, inequity and ethnic discrimination.

THE GREEK ORTHODOX ARCHDIOCESE
1972

One could not write about the history of
the Americans of Greek descent without
including a discourse on the role of the
church, describing the integral part it
has played in the lives of the Greek immigrants. The following article is an
excellent synopsis of the progress the
Greek Church experienced during the
fifty-year period extending from the establishment of the Archdiocese of North
and South America.

Source: 1972 Yearbook, pp. 10-13.

THE FIFTY YEARS OF LIFE AND DEVELOPMENT OF THE
GREEK ORTHODOX ARCHDIOCESE OF THE AMERICAS
1922 - 1972
An Appraisal
By
His Eminence Archbishop Iakovos

The above two dates represent a fifty-year period of time: the first
fifty years of our organized ecclesiastical life in America; a most
difficult task, still in progress. An organization entails our con-
forming to rules and regulations, thought and action - even in cases
where we ourselves are their authors. But discipline is hardly to
the liking of most of us; because we have never viewed it through
discipline; that is, in the nature of the discipline that we would
enforce upon ourselves. Discipline, in its nature of a call and
need, comes to us from "without" restricting and humiliating as
such would be. For this reason we observed that organization as
a task, an effort to enable both the individual and the group to
align themselves with certain national rules and regulations, is
still in progress. And it must necessarily continue in the future.
When some time ago (during the Royalist and Venizelists period),
the ecclesiastical life of the Greek-American people was interrupted,
this progressive organization found itself in "mortal danger," as the
result of divisions, bickering, fanaticism and hatred. These four
are "the powers of the darkness," constituting a negation of Chris-
tianity, by promoting a virtual abolishing of the Church as a spiri-

tual force and institution.

The first ten years of our Archdiocese, 1922-1932, was the period of "growing pains," the period of development from the embryonic state to childhood. Negative critics saw this period as a period of shame. Positive observers cannot fail to see it as a period of deep rooting in spite of the efforts of those whose "professed purpose is to uproot."

The ecclesiastical figure who began this ground-laying was Meletios Metaxakis. Alexander, the first canonical Archbishop of America, formerly Bishop of Rodostolon, reflected in his actions the genius of the former. The greatest of the acts of Metaxakis was his placing the Church of America under the jurisdiction of the Ecumenical Patriarchate, or rather, that he united the former with the Mother Church of all Orthodoxy.

This jurisdictional adjudging was dictated by necessity; by the necessity of survival. Else, the Church would not have survived in America. She was by far too nationalistic. Her leadership would have continued changing in accordance with the political changes of Greece. That was happening before Metaxakis. And would certainly continue happening after him if he were not far-sighted enough, if he did not have as much love as he did for the Greeks of America, and if he did not have the courage to become the founder of our Church.

Alexander fought courageously. If he lost heart and erred at the end of this painful decade, it was because every struggle has an end and a victim.

· The great service of Damaskenos, Metropolitan of Corinth and Exarch Extraordinary of the Ecumenical Patriarchate, consisted of his recommendation that Metropolitan Athenagoras become the successor of Alexander. Some believed at the time that this suggestion generated from personal reasons. But it would be a serious mistake to believe that Damaskenos suggested Athenagoras because he would prefer not to have him there as a potential adversary in seeking the throne of Athens. He suggested Athenagoras because he believed him to be the ablest from among the hierarchs there, to continue the organization of the Church in America.

Alexander's successor was a man of broad horizons, of broader heart, and of the broadest shoulders able to bear the very heavy burden of responsibilities that awaited him. Indeed, endowed with these qualities there was no one else but Athenagoras.

The nearly one score years of Athenagoras' tenure here - actually eighteen years, 1931-1949 - proved to be the greatest significance for the Greeks of America. First, because he gave them a feeling of self-respect. The boy immigrant of the first twenty years of the twentieth century was now a man, a husband, a father, a maker of himself, of his business, and above all these, the creator of his community and his Church. Second, because he instilled in them a feeling of responsibility; a new concept of responsibility for the Greek immigrant. The admonition of Athenagoras was that the Greeks of America should unite around the Church, a union which, if achieved, would make them conscientious Christians, respected by their American friends, and more valuable to their native Greece. Third, because he proved to them by his words, his eyes, and his deeds, the beauty, the personal happiness, and the creative force of love. He journeyed night and day, often in exhaustion, from one corner of America to another, thus personally witnessing to the Apostolic adage: "that which cometh upon me daily, the care of all the Churches." Fourth, because he made them believe in and face the reality and truth, that they were going to remain here; that they were to become the creators of a new Church; that they should decide to embark upon great endeavors, of the magnitude and scope of a Theological School and a Teachers' Training College. And finally, because he brought them in contact with the ecclesiastical and political authorities of their new country, with whom cooperation would prove to be essential to their own interest, in terms of their growth, and their assumption of a greater role in "the affairs of America."

The twenty years of Athenagoras marked the passing over from childhood to adolescence and from adolescence to manhood.

At this juncture, Archbishop Michael from Corinth entered the picture. He told our youth of 25-30 years old that it was their duty to prepare themselves to assume control of the government and progress of our communities.

The decade (1950-1960) of Michael's archiepiscopal tenure marked the changing over of the leadership of our communities from the old to the new generation. His greatest achievement was the creation of GOYA. Within this association the best from among our young men and women found a religious and cultural haven. Their circles generated not only enthusiastic youth leaders, religious instructors, community leaders, and excellent families, but the very hope and conviction that Orthodoxy can become, from an ecclesio-national personal identification tag, that it appeared to be, to a true religious experience of vital personal and group import.

During the historically significant archiepiscopal decade of Michael, the Greek-American youth acquired a sense of identification, the realization of their dual entity (Greek and American), and their first baptism of responsibility by being elected to the boards of trustees of our communities - to those select bodies of volunteer workers for Greek Orthodoxy in America.

But Archbishop Michael did not ignore another need· that the adult new generation concern themselves with our youngsters as well as with our pioneers in this country; to give direction and support to the young by way of Junior GOYA, to the pioneer - especially the lonely and aged - a home to live in and a shelter for his heart. The new generation did indeed give an organization to their own young within the bounds of the Greek Orthodox tradition, while the new clergymen gave a home to our aged. Thus, during Michael's decade the Omogeneia reached their maturity by assuming a number of responsibilities as it developed from generation to generation. Archbishop Michael's decade gave to the Greeks of America (by way of three generations) the feeling of an unbroken inner continuity.

Our fifth decade found us with this feeling of continuity well rooted in the hearts of our people. The problems of this decade began with the raising of our Church to her historic bright proscenium; with her becoming conscious of her ecumenical mission and role; with the task - which results in complete self-awareness of a mature Church - to unearth and unfold her possibilities. From "national" to become "above and beyond national," in the nature of our Ecumenical Patriarchate.

Greek-Americans have lived and still live with a commendable concern, with a concern about and care for their future. Apart from very few exceptions, all of them have lived with the dream of growth, with the unforseen always in view, with a preparation for unexpected adversity, with the deep desire not only to survive but to perpetuate what is their own. They believe and still believe that they have a kind of a mission that does not end at the grave; a mission of transforming the past into a live present, and the present into a dynamic future.

The fifth decade is the time of consolidating our gains, of embodying and investing our true values, and of the sacred handing down of the supreme charges and trusts we received from our glorious ancestry.

Which are the things we call our gains and possessions? All those hidden forces that contributed to the reaching of the Omogeneia to the very Ecumenical Throne by raising to it with their prayers Athenagoras I, the sublime; to the reaching of the White House where the voice of their Archbishop was raised in prayer at the inauguration of four Presidents (Eisenhower, Kennedy, Johnson, and Nixon); even to the Congress where they have five congressmen, and to the office of the very Vice President to which the son of a Greek immigrant was raised, Spiro Agnew.

Among the possessions, an important one is considered to be the status of the Omogeneia which is neither wholly Greek nor wholly American but Greek-American, a synthesis, strongly bound together and solidified to a degree that present circumstances would allow.

The values of the Omogeneia that await investment for the future are our religion, our Greek education, Greek culture and civilization, our love for our country, our ambition to survive, our determination

not to be blown to the four winds when the unavoidable storm will
lash one day our complex socio-cultural entity in this country. For,
mixed marriages will continue. Our concern should be how these
could be embodied in our Church and in our traditions, the guardian
of which is the very Church.

Our inherited historical charges and trusts consist in education,
in the upbringing of better future generations; in an unceasing effort
to reach the superior and better; in the command of our heritage to
keep nothing good exclusively for ourselves but to share it with
others and thus to multiply it.

From this brief analysis of the nature of "possessions, values
and ancestral charges and trusts" it must have become clear that
our Omogeneia have proceeded from their physical to their spiritual
growth. This has necessitated for us to "pain and sigh together"
an account of the difficult questions of this time, such as the
Greek language which is ignored, through no fault of the Omogeneia,
but because of the need to become familiar, if not its equal, with
the environment in which they live; such as the living of religion
not only as a national heritage but as the inner experience of a
spiritual life; such as mixed marriages that should become an opportunity for strengthening not weakening Orthodoxy; such as the upbringing of our children, of their education which should not draw
them away from our own circles since their membership in other
societies cannot supply them with the elements our culturo-religi-
ous circles could and should. Finally, we are concerned about the
terminal orientation of our children toward a combination of religious
and cultural values, common to both of our countries, seeing that a
double loyalty was proclaimed unrealistic and unnatural by Christ
Himself who stressed the fact that "no one can serve two masters
at the same time."

Our Omogeneia - and this is very consoling - thinks seriously
on these questions, even though there is no unanimous agreement
on interpreting them. And if they continue thinking responsibly,
they can and should reach the right decisions. The pulling in oppo-
site directions that is now played between "conservatives" and
"liberals" (one should grant good faith to both) should certainly
give way one day to a common and perhaps painful thinking-together
from which should issue not only the desirable, but mainly and
above all the realizable.

The fifth decade is the most well organized intellectually and
organizationally. But it should be so. The coming of age and development is part of a greater law. But this does not mean that our
organization is perfect. It merely indicates the existence and
strength of the Omogeneia, able to conform, in their great majority,
to law and right. The last two years, "years of crisis," testified
to the continuity and perserverance of the Omogeneia in the face of

all kind of trials and divisive activities. All that has been achieved
during the last decade - mainly in the educational, missionary,
ecumenical, administrative, and organizational quarters of our com-
munal and ecclesiastical life - testifies to the will, the strength,
and the insistence of the Omogeneia to continue and complete the
foundational work that was begun in 1922, and this against all
opposing efforts that existed in the past and still exist.

This brief analysis, which is actually a going back and a view-
ing from without of the "events" of the first fifty years of the life
and history of the Archdiocese, has not been written in the nature
of a festive article. It has been written with the purpose of direct-
ing the attention of the Greek-Americans from the surface to the
real depth of events. People, whether great or small in the eyes of
their fellow-men, bear a responsibility toward history and God: to
preserve "the sacred trust." And the sacred trust that was bequeath-
ed to us Greek-Americans by the will and hands of God Himself is
expressed in depth by the words with which an ordaining bishop ad-
monishes the new priest: "Preserve this sacred trust until the
second coming of the Lord Jesus Christ, at which time He will claim
it back from you."

We Greek-Americans - and this is unique in the history of our
people - have been the founders not merely of communities but of
ecclesiastical communities that became in the course of fifty years
a CHURCH. A Church with an identity, with stability, with spiritual and moral strength, with imposing stature, but above all, with
the unbroken unity that makes her a MAJOR FAITH. And this last is
the culminating point - the very expression - of the first fifty years
so abundantly and mercifully blessed by God.

And now our CHURCH is entering her second fifty years. If she
succeeds to remain, as it is validly hoped for, above all kinds of
arrangements and accommodations, our Church will prove the Body
of Christ; Christ Himself living for ever more. This is the service
that is expected of the coming generations of clergymen and laymen.
History will tell whether their faith will become witness, their witness courage, their courage truth, and the truth freedom; whether
their freedom will make them worthy and will forever redeem them
from delusionary fancies; thus, whether this last will become a new
Christian conscience which "from children of flesh and blood" will
transform them into generations born of God, in the midst of which
Christ, the truth and life, will prove the only truth of their own
lives.

UNITED HELLENIC AMERICAN
CONGRESS RESOLUTION
1976

Greek-American organizations throughout
the United States are greatly concerned
with the relationship between Greece and
Turkey and most specifically with the
problem of Cyprus. The following statement is a recent example of efforts to
inform Congress of the Greek-American
point of view.

Source: United States Congressional Record -
Extensions of Remarks, August 10, 1976,
p. E 4491.

HON. EDWARD J. DERWINSKI
of Illinois
In the House of Representatives
Tuesday, August 10, 1976

Mr. DERWINSKI. Mr. Speaker, I insert in the Record a resolution
adopted by the executive committee of the United Hellenic American
Congress, which met last month in Philadelphia.

The United Hellenic American Congress is a nationwide organization of Americans of Hellenic origin interested in developments
in this country as well as developments affecting Greece and Cyprus.
This group is a complete cross-section and has a truly representative
membership of the American-Greek community.

The resolution follows:

Resolution

Whereas, the United Hellenic American Congress has conducted
its National Meeting in the City of Philadelphia this 6th day of July,
1976, in conjunction with the observance of our country's Bicentennial celebration; and

Whereas, America has, from its inception, stood not only for
freedom, justice, and liberty for its people, but as a beacon of
freedom, justice, and liberty for all of the peoples of the world;

Now, therefore, be it resolved, that the Officers and Members
of the Executive Committee of the United Hellenic American Congress
assembled this 6th day of July, 1976, in the City of Philadelphia, do
hereby proclaim liberty and reaffirm our dedication to the principles
of the founding fathers of our Nation, and we hereby urge the Gov-

ernment of the United States to exert its full efforts and moral support for freedom and liberty and justice throughout the world; and

Be it further resolved, that the Congress of the United States is
hereby memorialized to continue to support democracy, self-determination, and majority rule throughout the world, and to condemn and
oppose aggression throughout the world; and

Be it further resolved, that the Congress of the United States is
hereby memorialized to continue support to the democracy in Greece
and to support the Rule of Law in prohibiting all arms transfers to
until Turkey withdraws all her troops and civilians from Cyprus and
allows all refugees to return to their homes.

A BICENTENNIAL STATEMENT - 1976

The United States celebrated its 200th birthday
in 1976, a celebration which was observed by
ethnic groups throughout America. The Americans of Greek descent were no exception. The
Archdiocese of North and South America for
example, chose the Bicentennial as the main
theme of their Yearbook. The article, reprinted
from the Yearbook, appearing below is one of
many statements made by American-Greeks in
observance of this historic event.

Source: 1976 Yearbook, p. 42.

the spirit of '76

Ernest A. Villas

In 1976 America celebrates her 200th
birthday commemorating the founding of a
free and independent United States. Unity
among the original colonies was a hard won
prize, for they were jealous of their states
rights and suspicious of federal authority.
Yet the eternal ideas molded into that
extraordinary document, the Declaration of
Independence: "We hold these truths to be
self evident: that all men are created equal,
endowed by their creator with certain
inalienable rights, that among these are life,
liberty and the pursuit of happiness . . . "
were destined to become the philosophical
foundation of the new Nation. From this
declaration grew the framework of the U. S.
Constitution, and later the Bill of Rights.
These immortal documents have served as a
model of nationhood for many peoples
seeking the freedom, public order and
human dignity that have become known as
"the American way of life." Indeed, even in
distant Greece the American revolution
served as a model that ignited the Greeks in
their struggle for freedom in 1821.

Nations are imperfect because mankind is
imperfect. Yet the remarkable 200-year
history of America has proven that people
can govern themselves, that the rule of law
is above the rule of men, and that truth and
equality ultimately do reside in the will of a
people who pledge themselves as "One
Nation, under God, with liberty and justice
for all."

The American people are comprised of
various groupings of religious bodies and
ethnic traditions. Like a mosaic of many
small tiles that make up the whole, America
is a reflection of many cultures and ways of
life. Our Greek Orthodox heritage is a
viable part of that mosaic. Unfortunately,
what has largely happened to our major
religious traditions in America, Catholic,
Protestant, Jewish and Orthodox, is that all
too often we are exactly as described above:
"colorful segments" in the mosaic of
American society rather than its inner
conscience. The terms "religion", "ethics",
"morality", "integrity", etc. should be
interlocking terms identifying the Church as

the public leaven of the society it serves. All too often it is not.

As Greek Orthodox we share the responsibility, even though our Greek Orthodox tradition is somewhat new on the American continent. From an administrative point of view we have been on the scene barely fifty years since the establishment of our Archdiocese in 1922. During the early years, and the previous decades when many of our Churches were founded, we were tolerated as immigrants, and sometimes looked upon as not-too-welcome "foreigners" from a distant land. Then came the period in which we were viewed as an ethnic and religious curiosity, with strange language, customs and religion, but tolerated and accepted. In the decades from the late '40's through the '50's Greek Orthodoxy spurted ahead on the American religious scene and became known, respected and ultimately accepted as the fourth major faith in America. Since then, the ever-increasing level of public dignity and respect for our Greek Orthodox tradition has grown to an almost disproportionate degree in comparison to our numbers. While this progress is due to many factors, the essential contributions can be attributed to the spiritual leadership of Archbishop Iakovos and many of our outstanding priests and laymen who have distinguished themselves on all levels of public and private life.

In our observance of the Bicentennial we are placed at a crossroads in American history that calls for more contemplation than celebration. Our inner conscience seems to be saying: "Yes, let us celebrate the past, but let us also take a hard look at ourselves as individuals, as a people, and as a Nation, spiritually, morally, intellectually, and physically, and then continue this renewing process as the years and decades roll by. In pledging ourselves to such a formula of ongoing renewal and introspection we will give our Bicentennial participation a dimension of dignity and truth that is truly worthy of this 200th anniversary of the United States of America.

A SALUTE TO THE ARCHDIOCESE BY
PRESIDENT GERALD R. FORD AND GOVERNOR
MILTON J. SHAPP-1976

The Archdiocese of North and South America
dedicated to Greek-Americans a commemorative book prepared for the Twenty-Third
Biennial Clergy-Laity Congress in 1976.
The following messages were contributed
by President Ford and Governor Shapp to
honor the opening of these meetings.

Source: <u>Twenty-Third Biennial Clergy-Laity</u>
<u>Congress</u> , 1976.

I am delighted to send greetings to the delegates at the
Twenty-Third Biennial Clergy-Laity Congress of the Greek
Orthodox Church in the Americas.

The city of Philadelphia provides an appropriate
historic setting for your meetings in this Bicentennial year. It
is the City of Brotherly Love—a cause to which you continue
to be dedicated as you perpetuate your inspiring religious
heritage.

This year we are more mindful than ever of the
great strength we have derived from the freedoms we cherish.
One of the greatest of these is the freedom of worship
which has enabled churches of all denominations to flourish
in our country and to serve our society.

The activities of the Greek Orthodox Church in
the Americas have been in the finest spirit of this religious
freedom and have greatly enriched us all. I welcome this
opportunity to wish you well in your sessions and to gratefully
acknowledge your important contribution to our national
vitality and well-being.

Gerald R. Ford
President of the United States

Americans of Greek descent have played an important role in helping America become a great nation. The people of Pennsylvania are fortunate to have many outstanding Greek–Americans who are making significant contributions in every field of human activity. Like so many other Americans, Greek settlers experienced many hardships, but they overcame all obstacles, thus making a better life for their families and the generations to come.

It is largely because of the determination and outstanding talents of people such as Americans of Greek descent that America is today a land of freedom, hope and productiveness.

Americans of Greek descent are fortunate as well to have as their spiritual leader one of this nation's outstanding clergymen, His Eminence, Archbishop Iakovos, a pillar of religious strength and wisdom.

As Governor of the Commonwealth of Pennsylvania, I extend to the many delegates and visitors and their families, who will assemble in Philadelphia during this historic week of July 2nd to July 9th, my best wishes for a successful and productive Congress.

Milton J. Shapp
Governor of Pennsylvania

GREEK-AMERICANS AND MUSIC - 1977

More and more Greek-Americans are becoming
involved in the cultural aspects of the American
society. The document below is an indication
of this cultural trend.

Source: News Release, Andel Management
Associates, New York.

GREEK CHORALE TOURS GREECE

Seventy singing ambassadors of the New York based Metropolitan
Greek Chorale, under the direction of their conductor, Dino Anagnost,
will depart on June 26th for a three week concert tour of Greece at
the invitation of the Greek government. The tour is being presented
under the High Patronage of His Eminence Archbishop Iakovos, Primate
of the Greek Orthodox Churches in the Americas.

Since its inception in 1966, the Metropolitan Greek Chorale, comprised of members from the Greek communities in the tri-state area,
has performed to capacity audiences with the highest critical praise
in Town Hall, Alice Tully Hall at Lincoln Center, Carnegie Hall, the
Maliotis Cultural Center in Boston, and other prestigious concert
halls throughout the east. This concert tour of Greece marks the
Chorale's European debut.

Acclaimed for its musical excellence and spirited renditions, the
Chorale has presented more than seventy-five concerts of Greek,
classical, semi-classical, and folk music, and has appeared with
many orchestras including the American Symphony Orchestra.

Under the musical direction of the young Greek-American conductor, Dino Anagnost, the Metropolitan Greek Chorale will appear at
several music festivals throughout Greece. Highlighting the Chorale's
summer program abroad will be performances on Rhodes and Crete, in
Athens and Salonika, and on national television. This concert tour
of Greece by the Metropolitan Greek Chorale and Dino Anagnost,
whose musical achievements are well known to American concert-
goers, will serve to forge a unique bond of communication between
the United States and Greece, where the word 'music' itself was born.

A LIST OF THE OLDEST GREEK ORTHODOX COMMUNITIES

IN NORTH AMERICA

WITH THE DATES OF THEIR ESTABLISHMENT

1.	New Orleans, Louisiana	1864
2.	New York City, New York	1892
3.	Chicago, Illinois	1892
4.	New York City, New York	1893
5.	Lowell, Massachusetts	1894
6.	Philadelphia, Pennsylvania	1901
7.	Birmingham, Alabama	1902
8.	Boston, Massachusetts	1903
9.	San Francisco, California	1904
10.	Newark, New Jersey	1904
11.	Washington, D.C.	1904
12.	St. Louis, Missouri	1904
13.	Milwaukee, Wisconsin	1904
14.	Providence, Rhode Island	1905
15.	Lynn, Massachusetts	1905
16.	Atlanta, Georgia	1905
17.	Savannah, Georgia	1905
18.	Montreal, Canada	1906
19.	Manchester, New Hampshire	1906
20.	Pittsburgh, Pennsylvania	1906

A LIST OF RENOWNED AMERICANS OF
GREEK DESCENT
1976
Taken From the Tribute to Greek-Americans in the Twenty-Third
Biennial Clergy-Laity Congress Commemorative Book

BUSINESS

CHRISTOS BASTIS, trustee of the Brooklyn Museum,
   owner of Seafare of the Aegean, New York.
TOM CARVEL, inventor of the Carvel Store.
JAMES GALANOS, fashion designer.
WILLIAM HELIS, JR., entrepreneur, one of the largest
   independent oil producers in the United States.
GEORGE LOIS, advertising executive.
PETER PETERSON, Secretary of Commerce, Chairman
   of Lehman Brothers.
EUGENE T. ROSSIDES, former Assistant Secretary of
   the Treasury, New York Lawyer.
SPYROS SKOURAS, Chairman of 20th Century Fox.
GEORGE STAVROPOULOS, fashion designer.
WILLIAM TAVOULAREAS, President, Mobil Corporation.
JOHN VERONIS, created the successful magazine,
   Psychology Today and now publishes Book Digest.
TED VERU, President of Publicker Distillers, Ltd.
NICOS ZOGRAPHOS, home and office designer.

SCIENCE

GEORGE C. COTZIAS, research on cancer.
PANAYOTIS KATSOYANNIS, insulin research.
JAMES NICHOLAS, Doctor for the Knicks and the Jets,
   research on the avoidance of athletic injuries.
GEORGE PAPANICOLOU, developed the "Pap Test"
   for detecting uterine cancer.

EDUCATION

MATINA SOURETIS HORNER, President of Radcliffe.
ANNE KARALEKAS, chosen to write the official history
   of the CIA.
EVANGELINE PAPAGEORGE, the Executive Associate
   Dean of Medicine at Emory University.

GEORGE VERONIS, helped start the prestigious Yale
School of Oceanography.

ENTERTAINMENT

THE ANDREW SISTERS, Maxene, Patty & Laverne,
popular singers.
CHARLIE CALLAS, comedian.
MARIA CALLAS, dramatic soprano of the opera.
JOHN CASSAVETES, actor, producer, director.
GEORGE CHAKIRIS, dancer, actor.
CHRISTOPHER GEORGE, actor.
ALEX KARRAS, past football player, now an actor and
television commentator.
GEORGE MAHARIS, actor.
DIMITRI MITROPOULOS, conductor.
IKE PAPPAS, news reporter for CBS.
TELLY A. SAVALAS, actor, star of the television pro-
gram, Kojak.
CAT STEVENS (Steven Georgiou), rock star, has been
awarded seven gold albums.
TATIANA TROYANOS, mezzo soprano of the opera.

THE ARTS

NICHOLAS GAGE, top investigative reporter for the
New York Times, top Mafia authority, has written
five books.
ELIA KAZAN, director of plays, academy award winning
director of movies, writer of novels.
HARRY MARK PETRAKIS, novelist.
ANDREW SARRIS, movie reviewer.
THEODOROS STAMOS, abstract painter.

GOVERNMENT

LEE ALEXANDER, Mayor of Syracuse, New York.
JOHN APOSTLE, Mayor of Annapolis, Maryland.
GEORGE ATHANSON, Mayor of Hartford, Connecticut.
HELEN BOOSALIS, Mayor of Lincoln, Nebraska.
JOHN BRADEMAS, Congressman from Indiana.
GEORGE CHRISTOPHER, Mayor of San Francisco,
California.
MICHAEL DUKAKIS, Governor of Massachusetts.
VICTOR KYRIAKIS, Mayor of Daly City, California.
JOHN MANOS, Mayor of Tenafly, New Jersey.

BRYON MATHEWS, Mayor of Newburyport, Massachusetts.
CYNTHIA MATHEWS, Mayor of Wethersfield, Connecticut.
JOHN NASSIKAS, former Chairman of the Federal Power
    Commission.
GEORGE ROUSAKIS, Mayor of Savannah, Georgia.
PETER SARANTO, Mayor of Elkhart, Indiana.
PAUL S. SARBANES, Senator from Maryland.
GUS YATRON, Congressman from Pennsylvania.

SPORTS

HARRY AGGANIS, baseball star.
BILLY LOES, baseball pitcher.
JIMMY LONDOS, wrestling's "Golden Greek".
DIANA NYAD, marathon swimmer.
MILT PAPPAS, baseball pitcher.
CHRIS PELEKOUDAS, National League Umpire.
PETER PIHOS, in two football Halls of Fame: College
    (Indiana) and Pro (Philadelphia Eagles).
LEAH POULOS, won a silver medal in the World Speed
    Skating Championship.
GUS TRIANDOS, baseball star.

OTHERS

PETE ATHAS
ALEX CAMPANIS
CHRIS FARASOPOULOS
BILL GEORGE
ALEX GRAMMAS
GEORGE KAFTAN
GUS NIARHOS
KATHERINE PAPPAS
LOU TSIOROPOULOS

GREEK NEWSPAPERS IN THE UNITED STATES

Daily

National Herald (Greek)   Publisher: B.J. Marketos
134 West 26th Street
New York, N.Y. 10001

Weeklies

Greek Press (English & Greek)   Editor: Aris Angelopoulos
505 N. LaSalle Street
Chicago, Ill. 60610

Greek Star (English and Greek)   Editor: Nicholas Philipiddis
4731 N. Western Avenue   Publisher: Andrew Fasseas
Chicago, Ill. 60625

Detroit Athens (Greek)   Editor: Basil Lukos
520 Monroe Avenue
Detroit, Mi. 48226

Greek Sunday News (Greek   Publisher: William Harris
and English)
231 Harrison Avenue
Boston, Mass. 02111

Hellenic Chronicle (English)   Publisher: Peter T. Agris
324 Newbury Street   Editor: James Anagnostos
Boston, Mass. 02115

Hellenic News   Andreas Papadonakis
117 West 57th Street
New York, N.Y. 10019

Hellenic Times   Editor & Publisher: Harry Stathos
1345 Third Avenue
New York, N.Y. 10021

National Greek Tribune   Editor & Publisher: James Lagos
1215 Brush Street
Detroit, Mi. 48226

GREEK NEWSPAPERS IN THE UNITED STATES

Semi-Weekly

Hellenic Voice   Mike Zapitis
22-74 31st Street
Astoria, N. Y. 11105

Bi-Weekly

Orthodox Observer (Greek and
English)   Publisher & Editor: P. Gazouleas
8 East 79th Street
New York, N.Y. 10021

The Hellenic Journal   Publisher: Frank P. Agnost
527 Commercial Street
San Francisco, Ca. 94111

Quarterly
Tribune of GAPA   Editor: Stavros Kalaras
3600 Fifth Avenue
Pittsburgh, Pa. 15213

GREEK PERIODICALS IN THE
UNITED STATES

Bi-Monthly

Ahepan Magazine (English)   Publisher: Order or AHEPA
1422 K Street, N.W.
Washington, D.C. 20005

Chicago PNYX (English)   Editor: Peter Mantzoros
Box 67
Glenview, Ill. 60025

Greek World   Editor: Emanuel Plaitakis
2039 Broadway
New York, N.Y. 10023

Monthly

Crete (Kriti)   (Greek and English)
30-43 36th Street   Publisher: Pancretan Assn. of America
Astoria, N. Y. 11103   Editor: George H. Terezakis

Greece
Greek Embassy - Cultural Division
2221 Massachusetts Ave., N.W.
Washington, D.C. 20008

Hellenic News   Editor: Savas Generalis
249 S. 10th Street
Philadelphia, Pa. 19107

New York (Greek and English)   Editor: Spiro Minotos
P.O.Box 675
Grand Central Station
New York, N.Y. 10017

PHOS   Editor: Efthihios Papagregorakis
26-80 30th Street
Astoria, N.Y. 11102

GREEK FEDERATIONS AND ORGANIZATIONS IN THE UNITED STATES

Aetoloakarnanon Society
Leonidas Lois, Pres.
44-08 47 Avenue
Woodside, N.Y. 11377

Allilovoithitikos Syllogos
Cyprion "Zinon"
Takis Loucas, Pres.
34-10 31st Avenue
Astoria, N.Y. 11103

Andros Society "Agios Philippos"
D. Mamais, Pres.
38-25 Parsons Blvd.
Flushing, N.Y.

Arkadian Association of America
Theodore Bouzalas, Pres.
8408 10th Avenue
Brooklyn, N.Y. 11209

Association of Hellenes from
Egypt of America
Archimidis Vasiliades, Pres.
P. O. Box 366
New York, N.Y. 10036

Athenian Society
Basil Georgalas, Pres.
13 Carmine Street
New York City 10014

Cassian Brotherhood
Nick King, Pres.
21-56 42nd Street
Astoria, N. Y.

Cephalonian Association
"Aenos"
P. Divaris, Pres.
307 W. 54th Street
New York, N.Y. 10019

Constantinople Society
Constantinos Sarantinos, Pres.
156 5th Avenue (R. 1206)
New York, N. Y. 10010

Cretan's Association "Omonoia"
George Lekanidis, Pres.
263 W. 30th Street
New York, N. Y. 10001

Cyprus Federation of America
Andrew Kornaris, Pres.
621 W. 172 Street
New York, N. Y. 10032

Epirotes Society "Anagennessis"
George Tsakalotos, Pres.
25-14 Broadway
Astoria, N. Y. 11106

Erikouson Brotherhood
Dr. Tasos Manesis, Pres.
211 E. 43rd Street
New York, New York 10017

Evritanon Society of America
"Evrytania"
Leonidas Tsatsaronis, Pres.
31-18 36th Street
Astoria, New York

Evrytanian Association of America
"Velouchi"
Tasos Tsaganos, S. Pres.
P. O. Box 394
Charlotte, N. C. 28201

Federation of American Hellenic
Societies in Greater New York Inc.
Dr. Michael Sideris, Pres.
200 E. 74th Street (Apt. 16 F)
New York, N. Y. 10021

GREEK FEDERATIONS AND ORGANIZATIONS IN THE UNITED STATES

Federation of Chian Society of
New York
George P. Livanos, Pres.
32-11 37th Street
Astoria, New York 11103

Federation of Dodecanese
Societies of America
Dr. Elia Horatazis, Pres.
422 Route 206 South
Somverville, N. J. 08878

Federation of Micraciatic and
Thracian Society of U.S.
and Canada
Kyriakos Mosaides, Pres.
420 W. Burne Drive
Broomall, Pa. 19008

Federation of Sterea Hellas
Tasos Tsaganos, Pres.
8919 North Elmore Street
Niles, Ill. 60648

G.A.P.A.
Nicholas Fakaris, S. Pres.
3600 Fifth Avenue
Pittsburgh, Pa. 15213

G.O.Y.A.
Nicholas Sakellariou,
National Chairman
1915 North 76th Avenue
Elmwood Park, Ill. 60635

Greek American Cyclades Island
Federation of America & Canada
Zannis Marmarinos, S. Pres.
116 Pinehurst Avenue
New York, N. Y. 10033

Greek Rumanian Association of
America
Basil Kordas, Pres.
240-28 67th Avenue
Douglaston, New York

Hellenic American Congress
Andrew Athens, Chairman
12900 South Metron Dr.
Lake Calumet Harbor
Chicago, Ill. 60633

Hellenic Cultural Circle "Filiko"
Dr. Demetrios Kotsilimbas, Pres.
133 E. 73rd Street
New York, N. Y. 10021

Hellenic Medical Society
Dr. Marinos Petratos, Pres.
P. O. Box 337, F.D.R. Station
New York, New York 10022

Hellenic Universities Graduates
Association, Inc.
Dr. George Kokotakis, Pres.
30-02 30th Drive
Astoria, New York 11102

Hellenic University Club
Basil Exarchos, Pres.
P.O.Box 1169 Grand Central Stat.
New York, N. Y. 10017

Hydras Society
Stamatios Kalafatis, Pres.
601 W. 189th Street
New York, N. Y. 10040

Kastelorizoton Society
Michael Savas, Pres.
146-52 28th Avenue
Flushing, N.Y. 11354

GREEK FEDERATIONS AND ORGANIZATIONS IN THE UNITED STATES

Kastorian Society
George Kaiteris, Pres.
246-8th Ave. (Kastorian Bldg.)
New York, N.Y. 10011

"Kefalos" Society
Denis Konstantakis, Pres.
32-34 72nd Street
Jackson Heights, N.Y.

Lacedemonians Association
Eleftherios Vouyouklis, Pres.
149 Bay 44th Street
Brooklyn, N. Y. 11214

Messinian Benevolent
"Aristomenis"
Nicholas Tzavaras, Pres.
160-10 84th Road
Jamaica, N. Y. 11432

Monemvasioton Society
Vasilios Broutzas, Pres.
23-62 35th Street
Astoria, N. Y. 11105

Naupaktians Brotherhood
Trifon Hatzinikolaou, Pres.
242 Beach 124 Street
Rockaway Park, N.Y. 11694

New York Greek Society
Vryseon Anavrytis
Perry Chrysomalis, Pres.
44-26 65th Street
Woodside, N. Y. 11377

Nisyrian Society "Gnomagoras"
Nicholas Sakalis, Pres.
23-18 29th Street
Astoria, New York 11105

Nisyrian Society "St. John
Theologos"
Stavros Hartofilis, Pres.
43-01 Broadway
Astoria, New York 11103

Order of A.H.E.P.A.
Xenophon Microutsicos, S. Pres.
Supreme Lodge Headquarters
1442 "K" St. N.W.
Washington, D.C. 20006

Panahaian Benevolent "Agia Lavra"
Danny Pappas, Pres.
c/o T. Kandaras
670 9th Avenue
New York, N.Y. 10036

"Panagia Proussiotissa"
Allilovoithtikos Syllogos
Andreas Katsanos, Pres.
250 W. 57th Street (s.314)
New York, N.Y. 10019

Panarcadian Federation of America
Leo Lamberson, Pres.
8711 S. Ridgeland Avenue
State Road Plaza
Oaklawn, Ill. 60453

Pan-Coan Society "Hippocrates"
Nicholas G. Itsines, Pres.
471 Broadway
Staten Island, N.Y. 10310

Pancretan Association of America
Emmanual Tsourounis, S. Pres.
12330 Hatton Point Road
Tantallon, Md. 20022

GREEK FEDERATIONS AND ORGANIZATIONS IN THE UNITED STATES

Panepirotic Federation of America
Dr. Basil Photos, S. Pres.
2324 W. Lawrence Avenue
Chicago, Ill. 60625

Pan-Elian Federation
Fotios Plakogiannis, S. Pres.
104-20 Queens Blvd. Apt. 19H
Forest Hills, N. Y. 11375

Paneuboean Society
D. Xypolias, Pres.
22-33 33rd Street
Astoria, N. Y.

Panicarian Brotherhood Icaros
Jack Kozamanis, Pres.
1243 Edward Street
Lakewood, Ohio 44106

Panhiaki Society "Koraes"
Stelios Tatsis, Pres.
Koraes Building
5814 Roosevelt Ave.
Woodside, N. Y. 11377

Panimbrian Benevolent Society
George Aneson, Pres.
540 81st Street
Brooklyn, N.Y. 11209

Panlaconian Society
Paraskevas Michaei, S. Pres.
10140 Southerland Road
Silver Springs, Md. 20091

Panlemnian Society "Hyfestos"
Nick Giannopoulos, Pres.
35-20 28th Street
Astoria, N.Y. 11106

Panlesvian Society of America
Constantine Stamboulis, S. Pres.
141 89th Street
Brooklyn, N. Y. 11209

Panmacedonian Association
Peter Mitoulis, S. Pres.
370 7th Avenue
New York, N. Y. 10001

Panmessinian Federation
Dan Terzakis, Pres.
2917 W. 95
Evergreen, Ill. 60642

Panrhodian Repr. in New York
Stylianos Giamalis
29 Brookvale Lane
Lake Grove, N. Y. 11755

Pansamian Federation
Xenophon Papageorge, Pres.
P.O.Box 02290
Cleveland, Ohio 44102

Panthessalian Federation
Theodore Diamantopoulos, S. Pres.
2411 1st Street
Fort Lee, N. J. 07027

Piraikos Benevolent Association
Constantine Kotleakos, Pres.
350 E. 67 Street
New York, N. Y. 10021

Pontion Society
John Papadopoulos, Pres.
31-25 23rd Avenue
Astoria, N. Y. 11105

GREEK FEDERATIONS AND ORGANIZATIONS IN THE UNITED STATES

Panrhodian Society of America
Philip Anastasiadis, S. Pres.
401 South Garfield Street
Arlington, Va. 22204

Panhellenic Seamens Ass'n.
Spyros Varras, Pres.
Fisk Bldg. 250 W. 57 St.
New York, N. Y. 10019

Samos Society "Phythagoras"
George Vrotsos, Pres.
111-02 39th Avenue
Corona, N. Y. 11368

Society of Macedonians
"Aliakmon"
Erakis Tsiolas, Pres.
352 7th Avenue
New York, N. Y. 10001

Thessalonikians Society of
St. Demetrios & Lefkos Pyrgos
Sotirios Proios, Pres.
363 7th Avenue
New York, N. Y. 10001

Theveon Society "Epaminondas"
Panagiotis Dedes, Pres.
161 Route 46 East
Lodi, N. J. 07644

United Chios Society of America
John Kellis, Pres.
20 Hiddenwood Estates
Stewbenville, Ohio 43952

United Cypriots of America
Dr. Costas Elias
28-16 Astoria Blvd.
Astoria, N. Y. 11102

Vorioepiroton Pyrrhus
Benevolent Society
Christos Mikelis, Pres.
307 W. 54th Street
New York, N. Y. 10019

Zakinthion Brotherhood
Danny Pappas, Pres.
515 83rd Street
Brooklyn, N. Y. 11209

BIBLIOGRAPHY

The selective bibliography that follows suggests the vast amount of literature on the Greeks in America that is available to the ardent researcher. The list is not comprehensive, rather it is offered as a starting point for students interested in examining from an historical perspective the development of Greek emigration to the United States and in discovering the progress made by the Greek communities in America. Although the bibliography lists a great many useful reference tools, we commend two volumes for special mention here. *The Greeks in the United States* by Theodore Saloutos (Harvard University Press, 1964) we found to be both comprehensive and well written, and as such, our most valuable work of reference. In particular, it is recommended for its coverage of the period between 1915 and 1945. For its examination of the earliest period of Greek immigration to the United States, of noteworthy stature is the volume by E.P. Panagopoulos, *New Smyrna: An Eighteenth Century Greek Odyssey* (University of Florida Press, Gainesville, 1966). It is a scholarly book, and yet it holds the reader's interest, a combination greatly appreciated by the researcher.

BIBLIOGRAPHY

BIBLIOGRAPHY

Primary Sources

Adamic, Louis. "Americans from Greece." A Nation of Nations.
New York: Harper, 1945. This historical overview of the Greek-
American experience includes short biographical sketches and
lists prominent Greek-Americans in the arts, sciences, and
business.

Burgess, Thomas. Greeks in America: An Account of their Coming,
Progress, Customs, Living and Aspirations. Boston: Sherman,
French and Company, 1913; reprint New York: Arno Press, 1975.
Covers early immigration of Greeks, especially the Greek organi-
zations and the Greek Orthodox Church.

Choukas, Michael. "Greek Americans." Our Racial and National
Minorities. Eds. Francis J. Brown and Joseph Slabey Roucek.
New York: Prentice Hall, 1937, pp. 339-357. Surveys causes
of emigration, occupations in the United States, religion, education, fraternal organizations, the Greek-American press, the
contributions of the Greeks to America, with bibliography.

Doggett, Carita. Dr. Andrew Turnbull and The New Smyrna Colony
of Florida. Florida: The Drew Press, 1919. The book is written
by a direct descendant of Dr. Turnbull, written mostly in his
defense, but has some interesting information.

Fairchild, Henry Pratt. "The Greeks." Immigrant Backgrounds.
New York: Wiley, 1927.

Greek Orthodox Yearbooks. Archdiocese of North and South America. Contain useful information regarding church activities.

Lacey, Thomas James. A Study of Social Heredity as Illustrated in
the Greek People. New York: Gorham, 1916. Considers Ancient
Greece, Modern Greece, and the Greeks in America, to discover
continuing social patterns. Section on Greeks in America includes a sketch on immigration, unifying influences, and individual Greek communities in New York, Chicago, Lowell,
Massachusetts, and Tarpon Springs, Florida.

U.S. Department of Commerce and Labor. Emigration to the United States.

Valaoras, Vasileos. Hellenism of the United States. Athens, Greece· Leoni, 1937. Written in Greek but with an English preface and summary by M.C. Balfour. Based on his observations while in the United States as a fellow of the Rockefeller Foundation, Valaoras' study finds that Greeks are being assimilated into the larger American population. There are 2.84 males to every 1 female in the Greek immigrant group, 45% of Greeks in the United States have adopted citizenship, and 90% have learned English. There are 242 Greek Orthodox churches and over 400 Greek schools. The author hopes that Greek-Americans adopt what is best in American culture and also preserve the best values of their Hellenic heritage.

Vlachos, Evangelos. The Assimilation of the Greek in the United States. Athens, Greece: Publications of the National Centre of Social Researches, 2, 1968. Examines the emerging Greek-American culture which accomodates traditional Greek cultural patterns to American reality, and considers the extent to which third-generation Greek-Americans identify with this culture. Studies Greek-American communities nation-wide, but with particular emphasis on the one community. Based on the author's Ph.D. dissertation, with the same title, prepared at Indiana University in 1964.

Vlavianos, Basil J. "Greek Americans." One America. Eds. Francis James Brown and Joseph Slabey Roucek. New York· Prentice-Hall, 1937; 3rd ed., New York: Prentice-Hall, 1952, pp. 239-244. Surveys Greek immigration, with sections on "Cultural differentiation" and "Contributions to American Life." Especially good on early immigration.

Vournas, George C. "Greeks in America." Congressional Record: Proceedings and Debates of the 86th Congress, 2nd Session. Washington, D.C., 1960. Appendix pp. A137-A142.

Woodhead, Arthur Geoffrey. The Greeks in the West. London· Thames & Hudson, 1962.

Xenides, J.P. The Greeks in America. New York: Doran, 1922; rpt. San Francisco: R. & E Research Associates, 1972. With an introduction by Charles Hatch Sears. Appeared under the auspices of the Inter-Church World Movement. A good history of the Greek presence in America up to the time of its publication.

Stresses relations between the Greek Orthodox Church and the
Protestant churches of the United States. Includes a section on
the European background of the Greek emigration and a useful
appendix on Greek newspapers in the United States.

Zotos, Stephanos. Hellenic Presence in America. Wheaton, Ill.:
Pilgrimage, 1976. A good overall account of Greek immigrants
to America from the beginning to the present.

Secondary Sources

Abbott, Grace. "Study of the Greeks in Chicago." American Journal
of Sociology, 15 (November 1909), 379-393. Based on the
Hull House Study of 1908, it concludes that the Greek is a desirable immigrant because he is trained in democracy and he
quickly establishes himself in a small business. (see document
this vol.)

Adamic, Louis. "Greeks Came to Tarpon Springs." From Many Lands.
New York: Harper, (1940), pp. 116-131. Account of the birth
and growth of the sponge fishing industry in Tarpon Springs,
Florida.

Adeney, Walter F. The Greek and Eastern Churches. New York:
Sribner's, 1908. Detailed history in two parts, the first giving
the history of the "main body of the church throughout the Eastern
provinces of Christendom," and the second part giving a history
of each of the separate churches after they break with the main
body.

Anderson, Paul B. "Eastern Orthodox Churches in the United States."
Information Service, 34, No. 43 (Saturday, December 24, 1955)

Andreades, A. "The Currant Crisis in Greece." Economic Journal,
16 (1906), 41-51. Deals with events after 1899, especially
with the bill of 1905 and the convention which it sanctioned.

Antoniou, Mary. "Welfare Activities Among the Greek People in Los
Angeles." Master's thesis, University of Southern California,
1939. Includes a map of Los Angeles' "Greek-town," as well as
a comprehensive bibliography.

Athenagoras, Bishop. "Holy Cross Greek Orthodox Theological
School: Twenty Years of Progress, 1937-1957." The Greek
Orthodox Theological Review, 3 (1957), 15-22.

Boardman, John. The Greeks Overseas. Harmondsworth, England, and Baltimore, Maryland: Penguin, 1964.

Booras, H. J. Hellenic Independence and America's Contribution to the Cause. Rutland, Vermont, 1935. Part I is a history of the war for Hellenic independence; Part II is an account of America's contribution to the war effort.

Brown, Carroll N. "Shall the Children of Greek Americans Learn Greek?" Hellenic Spectator, 1, No. 3 (May 1940), 3-4.

Boyd, Rosamonde R. The Social Adjustment of the Greeks in Spartan-burg, South Carolina. Spartanburg, South Carolina: William Printing Company, 1949. Research conducted under a grant from the Carnegie Foundation.

Bruce, Karen S. "The Social Organization of the Greek Community in Minneapolis." Manuscript in the Center for Immigration Studies, University of Minnesota, n.d.

Calodikes, C.S. The Golden Book, or The Greek and American Spirit. New York, 1917; 2nd ed., New York, 1923. Includes President Wilson's address to Congress on April 2, 1917, and "The Cy-clops," a satyric drama translated from the Greek by Shelley.

Calogeropoulos, N., and G. Stratos. Notes on the Greek Question: Addresses to President Wilson. 1920.

Casavis, Jack N. Children of the Sun. New York: Dodecanesian League of America, 1942. Also published by the Dodecanesian League are six pamphlets written by the same author giving the history of the Dodecanesian Greeks and a plea for their liberation.

Coburn, Frederick W. History of Lowell and Its People. Vol. 2. New York: Lewis Historical Publishing Company, 1920.

Constant, Theodore N. "Employment and Business of the Greeks in the United States." Athene, 6 (Winter 1945) 37-39; 7 (Sum-mer 1946), 40-41;(Autumn 1946), 28-29; 7 (Winter 1947), 37-41, 46.

_____. "Greek-American Colonies, Churches and Schools in the United States." Athene, 11 (Autumn 1950), 26-27; 11 (Winter 1951), 12-23, 54; 12 (Spring 1951), 34-35, 50.

_____. "Problems of Greek-Americans." Athene 12 (1951), 29-30, 60-64; No. 4, 22-24; 13 (1952), No. 1, 28-29, 56-58.

_____. "Racial Prejudice and the Greek Stock in the United States." Athene, 5 (Autumn 1944), 8-11.

Constantelos, Demetrios J. The Greek Orthodox Church: Faith, History, and Practice. New York: Seabury, 1967. A good introduction to the teachings and ethos of the Greek Orthodox Church. Intended for the layman, both Orthodox and non-Orthodox.

Cooke, T. S. "The Greeks in the Unted States." Eastern and Western Review, 3 (November 1910). This survey was written during the peak of immigration.

Corse, Carita, and the Florida Writers Project. "Greek-Americans of Florida." Athene, 3 (1942), No. 5, 17-21; No. 6, 22-25, 29; No. 7, 22-26; No. 8, 10-12, 15; No. 9, 10-12; No. 10, 14-15; 4 (1943), No. 2, 12-13; No. 3, 10-11, 13.

Doukas, Kimon   "The Story of Ahepa." Athene, 11 (Summer 1950), 39-43.

Doumouras, Alexander. "Greek Orthodox Communities in America Before World War I." St. Vladimir's Seminary Quarterly, 11 (1967), 172-192.

Ellis, Leonora B. "Harvest of the Sea Floor — Sponge Gathering by the Largest Unmixed Greek Community in America." Natural History, 41 (January 1938), 62-66.

"The Forgotten Generation." Athene, 10 (1950), 22-23, 41-42.

Frantsis, George T. Strangers at Ithaca: The Story of the Spongers of Tarpon Springs. St. Petersburg, Florida: Great Outdoors, 1962.

Georgas, Demitra. "Greek Settlement of the San Francisco Bay Area." Master's thesis, University of California at Berkeley, June, 1951.

"The Greeks in America." Literary Digest, 49 (December 7, 1918), 37.

The Greeks in California, Their History and Achievements, 1918-1919. San Francisco: Prometheus, 1919.

Harris, Jennie E. "Sponge Fisherman of Tarpon Springs." National Geographic Magazine, 91 (January 1947), 119-136.

Hunt, Milton B. "The Housing of Non-Family Groups of Men in Chicago." American Journal of Sociology, 16 (1910), 145-171.

Kallimachos, Demetrios. "Greek College in America." Argonautes, A (1959), 43-48. Argument against such a college.

Kourides, Peter T. The Evolution of the Greek Orthodox Church in America and Its Present Problems. New York: Cosmos Greek-American Printing Company, 1959.

Lagoudakis, Charilaos. "Greeks in Michigan." Michigan History Magazine, 14 (1930), 15-27. Describes the help sent by Detroit to Greece during her War of Independence, and the naming of Ypsilanti after the Greek hero.

Lauck, W. Jett. "Industrial Communities." Survey 25 (January 7, 1911), 579-586. Study of immigrant groups in industrial communities.

Lauquier, Helen Capanidou. "Cultural Change Among Three Generations of Greeks." American Catholic Sociological Review, 22 (1961), 223-232.

Loukas, Christ. "Status of Greek Population in the United States." The Hellenic Spectator, 1, No. 1 (February 1940), 3-9.

_____. United States Population of Greek Origin, First and Second Generation, United States Census 1930. New York: Department of Sociology, Columbia University, n.d.

Maisel, Albert Q. "The Greeks Among Us." Reader's Digest, 67 July 1955, 113-118.

Marshall, Grace E. Eternal Greece. Rochester, New York: Dubois, 1938. Concerned with motivations that led Greeks to emigrate.

Nelson, Lowry. "Speaking of Tongues." American Journal of Sociology, 54 (1948), 202-210.

Paleologas, Emmaline. I Married a Greek. Mansfield, Ohio· Stirling, 1941. Account by an English girl of her trip to Greece with her husband, with observations on political and refugee situation.

Politis, M.J. "Greek-Americans." One America. Eds. Francis J. Brown and Joseph Slabey Roucek. New York: Prentice-Hall, 1945, pp. 242-257. General history of Greek immigration, life in the

United States, assimilation, and contribution to America.

Politopoulos, Takes E. "Maniates in America." Nea Easta, 50 (September 1951), 580. Concerned with Greeks who came to New Smyrna, Florida, with Dr. Andrew Turnbull in 1767.

Rosen, Bernard C. "Race, Ethnicity, and the Achievement Syndrome." American Sociological Review, 24 (1959), 47-60.

Rothchild, Constantina Safilios. Survey of Sociologists who have completed or are working on Greek-Americans, 1968. Detroit: Merrill-Palmer Institute. Continuing research.

Seaman, Paul David. Modern Greek and American English in Contact. The Hague: Mouton, 1972. Study of the Modern Greek Language in America, examining social and cultural factors influencing Greek-Americans.

Saloutos, Theodore. They Remember America: The Story of the Re-patriated Greek-Americans. Berkeley, California: University of California Press, 1956. Bibliography included.

Smith, Mapheus. "National Origins of Prominent Immigrants." Sociology and Social Research, 20 (1936), 422-432.

Spiegel, John P. "Cultural Value and Mental Health in Greek-American Families." Brockton, Mass.: Veterans Adminstration Hospital, 1963, 1966.

Stephanides, Marios. The Greeks in Detroit: Authoritarianism — A Critical Analysis of Greek Culture, Personality, Attitudes and Behavior. San Francisco: R. & E. Research Associates, 1975.

Stycos, Mayone J. "The Spartan Greeks of Bridgetown: Community Cohesion." Common Ground, 8 (Winter 1948), 61-70; (Spring 1948), 24-34; (Summer 1948), 72-86.

Terhune, Leoloa Benedict. "Greek Bootblack." Survey, 26 (September 16, 1911), 852-854. Describes plight of Greek boys working long hours for slave wages and suggests that other cities follow the lead of Lowell, Mass., and pass an ordinance requiring illiterate minors to attend night school.

Theodoratus, Robert James. "The Influence of the Homeland on the Social Organization of a Greek Community in America." Doctoral dissertation, University of Washington, 1961.

Treudley, Mary B. "Formal Organization and the Americanization Process, with Special Reference to the Greeks of Boston." American Sociological Review, 14 (1949), 44-53.

Turnbull, Andrew. "The Refutation of the Late Account of New Smyrna." Columbian Magazine (November 1788). Dr. Turnbull's own defense of his conduct in administering the Greek-American colony at New Smyrna, Florida.

Walker, Natalie. "Chicago Housing Conditions. Greeks and Italians in the Neighborhood of Hull House." American Journal of Sociology, 21 (1915), 285-316.

Warner, W. Lloyd, and Leo Srole. The Social System of American Ethnic Groups. New Haven, Connecticut: Yale University Press, 1945.

Weinberger, Helen. "A Study of the Assimilation of Foreign-Born Greeks in Cincinnati, Ohio." Master's thesis, University of Cincinnati, 1942.

Wiest, Walter E. "The Centenary of the Greek Orthodox Archdiocese of North and South America." The Orthodox Ethos: Studies in Orthodoxy. Ed. A. J. Philippou. Oxford, England: Holywell, 1964. Vol. 1, 3-20.

Xanthaky, Socrates Anthony. The Greeks' Companion. New York: The Atlantis, 1903. Guide for the Greek immigrant to life in the United States and Canada. Greek and English text.

Zirpiades, Fotine. "Portrait of Papa." Common Ground, 4 (1943), 80-85. Fond reminiscence by a second generation Greek-American of her immigrant father, his pride, his difficulty pronouncing English, his financial success won through hard work as a boot-black and as the owner of a hat store.

_____. "Sophia Becomes an American." Common Ground, 4 (1944), 97-102. Account of Sophia Andreopoulos' learning to speak English and gaining citizenship after much shyness, fear, and prodding by the family.

Official Documents

United States 61st Congress, 3rd Session, Senate Document No. 747. Abstracts of the Reports of the Immigration Commission, 2. Washington, D.C.: U.S. Government Printing Office, 1911.

United States 61st Congress, Senate Document No. 753, Reports of the Immigration Commission. Immigrant Banks. Washington, D.C.: U.S. Government Printing Office, 1911.

United States 61st Congress, Senate Document No. 756, Reports of the Immigration Commission. Statistical Review of Immigration, 1820-1910. Washington, D.C.: U.S. Government Printing Office, 1911.

United States 67th Congress, 2nd Session, Senate Document No. 86. Loans to Foreign Governments. Washington, D.C.: U.S. Government Printing Office, 1921.

United States 81st Congress, 2nd Session, Senate Report No. 1515. The Immigration and Naturalization Systems of the United States. Washington, D.C.: U.S. Government Printing Office, 1950.

United States 82nd Congress, 2nd Session House of Representatives. Hearings Before the President's Commission on Immigration and Naturalization. Washington, D.C.: U.S. Government Printing Office, 1952.

United States 83rd Congress, 2nd Session. First Semiannual Report of the Administration of the Refugee Relief Act of 1953. Washington, D.C.: U.S. Government Printing Office, 1954.

United States 85th Congress, 1st Session. Refugee Relief Act of 1953, Final Report of the Administrator of the Refugee Relief Act of 1953, As Amended. Washington, D.C.; U.S. Government Printing Office, 1956.

United States Department of Commerce and Labor, Bureau of Naturalization. Annual Reports of the Commissioner of Naturalization, 1918, 1923-1932, 1944, 1952, 1960.

United States Department of Commerce and Labor, Bureau of Statistics. Special Consular Reports. Emigration to the United States. Washington, D.C.: U.S. Government Printing Office, 1903.

United States 49th Congress, 2nd Session, House of Representatives, Executive Document No. 157, Emigration and Immigration. Reports of the Consular Officers of the United States.
Washington, D.C.: U.S. Government Printing Office, 1887.